DOVES & DASEIN

WRITTEN BY

JEREMY FORSYTHE

AN ANTHOLOGY OF APHORISMS,
A BRIEF HISTORY OF THE SAOL,
DASEIN, SUICIDE, & BEAUTY.

DOVES AND DASEIN ©

First edition published in 2018

ISBN-13:   978-1-9994229-0-5
ISBN-10:   1999422902

Author
Jeremy Forsythe

Cover Design
Jeremy Forsythe

Editor
Alexandria Melone

CINDY

IS AIT AN MAC AN SAOL

LIFE IS STRANGE

CONTENTS

THE PHILOSOPHER OF DASEIN

Why are there beings at all instead of nothing? That is the question. Presumably it is no arbitrary question. "Why are there beings at all instead of nothing?"—this is obviously the first of all questions. Of course, it is not the first question in the chronological sense. Individuals as well as peoples ask many questions in the course of their historical passage through time. They explore, investigate, and test many sorts of things before they run into the question "Why are there beings at all instead of nothing?" [...] And yet, we are each touched once, maybe even now and then, by the concealed power of this question, without properly grasping what is happening to us. In great despair, for example, when all weight tends to dwindle away from things and the sense of things grows dark, the question looms. Perhaps it strikes only once, like the muffled tolling of a bell that resounds into Dasein and gradually fades away. The question is there in heartfelt joy, for then all things are transformed and surround us as if for the first time, as if it were easier to grasp that they were not, rather than that they are, and are as they are. The question is there in a spell of boredom, when we are equally distant from despair and joy, but when the stubborn ordinariness of beings lays open a wasteland in which it makes no difference to us whether beings are or are not— and then, in a distinctive form, the question resonates once again: Why are there beings at all instead of nothing?

—MARTIN HEIDEGGER

Introduction to Metaphysics, 1953

THE BEGINNING

This anthology of aphorisms is my attempt to fulfill the Saol dictum, *that to justify, and thus transcend the suffering of one's existence, one has to create, disseminate, and become something beautiful.*

Last year, I had the distinct honour of staying with the Saol at their compound for seven days and seven nights. During my stay, I could not fully comprehend the profundity of what this peculiar set of people had taught—even though, when they had taught, they did so with great fervor. Nevertheless, a seed was planted—and this book serves as proof of the fully blossomed flower this small seed had birthed.

The purpose of this book will be twofold.

First will be to provide you with a glimpse into the well of my thoughts, ideas, fears, wishes, hopes, and memories. In short, to encapsulate in words, as best I can, my experience being human in the world. In this, I hope that you will discover a common thread—that life, with all its suffering, is worth living. As you read, it will be important to note that two separate timelines exist within this book in which these aphorisms were written—those that were written before my trip to the Saol compound, and those that were written after my departure. These separate timelines are marked by a distinct shift in consciousness—namely, a shift in my perception of the world and my place within it. I will leave it up to you, the reader, to place each aphorism into their respective timeline, and further, to decipher any accompanying shift in consciousness that has not already been stated.

Second will be to disseminate the message of the Saol people—a message that originated at the hands of a single man—the one the Saol call the 'Master.' The Saol is an isolated colony cut off from the Western world. To this end, I have made it a personal and moral duty to carry their way of life overseas, bringing their message close to the people I hold dearest to my heart—the people of the modern world. For this reason, you will find an outline of the Saol history and their nine celebrated epiphanies weaved throughout these aphoristic pages—and my hope is that you will find these epiphanies as transformative as I have.

As a result, the sections entitled *History of the Saol* must be read in order, starting from *Part I* to *Part IX,* then from *The First Epiphany* to *The Final Epiphany*, then finally, the Saol history and the story of my sojourn comes to a close with the sections entitled *A Way of Life, My Departure from the Saol Compound, A Small Seed,* and *The End.* However, my aphorisms may be read in whatever way serves you.

My admittedly inadequate education regarding the history of the Saol had been elucidated during my stay at the compound, by a very gracious Saol guide. In the pages that follow, I will attempt to reiterate his speech and the Saol lessons as best as memory serves.

HISTORY OF THE SAOL

PART I

HISTORY OF THE SAOL: PART I

Both the Saol guide and I sat comfortably at a long, wooden table that stretched double the size of any table I had ever seen. It was an imposing slab of dark oak—polished and exceptionally carved.

At the head of the impressive table hung a large canvas print of the Henri Matisse painting, *Joy of Life*.

We ate, we drank, we talked—and only through our subsequent discussion on the history of the Saol did I come to realize that this painting stood as a perfect representation of the colony's guiding ethos.

My gracious guide then began.

"The history of the Saol began under precarious circumstances, circumstances that trail back many decades ago, to a single man of enigmatic origins. It is true that Amhrán—the current head of the Saol colony—is the last of us alive to have interacted with this man—and still, only a handful of the earliest Saol people had ever seen him, talked to him, or heard him speak—all of whom have long since passed. We call this enigmatic figure the *Master*. It is through his undying efforts that this compound, this colony, and the Saol way of life came to be.

"And yet, it is said that after the Master established the Saol colony, he vanished from the compound without having seen it flourish—with people travelling the world over to devote themselves to, and ultimately fulfill, the Saol dictum.

"Amhrán tells us that the Master hadn't any further need of the compound—for the Master had *created,* and a wave of peace and joy overtook his mind, permanently transforming his *Being.*

"That is, because the Master had finally answered that question, *in the positive*—the question that we all must answer—the one, over there, written above *Joy of Life*."

The guide then pointed to a question etched in gold lettering, written on a beautiful plaque above *Joy of Life*. It read: *'Is Being better than Nothing?'*

This is of the grandest of moral questions—one that raged a violent storm within my mind, crashing down thunderous bolts of lightning upon all that I knew, upon all that I was. It is true that a great philosopher of antiquity once asked the ontological question: *'Why are there beings at all instead of nothing?'* But, how much more important it is to ask its moral equivalent.

How it is that I came upon the Saol was by a series of fortuitous, yet favourable circumstances. And yet, if it wasn't for my encounter with Amhrán—the Saol leader, and the last among the Saol to have seen the Master—I wouldn't have it in me to tell you of this story.

I owe Amhrán my life. I owe the Saol my life. It is they who had nourished me with a guiding principle. My hope now is to nourish you with that very same seed.

DOVES AND DASEIN

I look out the window
and see a dove
dancing in the grass.
The dove effortlessly dances
the dance of Being.
Humans are different.
It is hard for humans to dance
the dance of Being,
for the human is in a
constant questioning of
the dance itself.

DUKKHA

Suffering is an inextricable
feature of human existence.

To speak of a *human*
is to implicitly admit of
this being *that it has suffered.*

Is it not the case that our very birth
was our first confrontation with suffering?

Our helpless gasping for first breath
to stave off the pang of virgin lungs,
our non-consensual abduction from
the comfortable home of our mother's womb,
our first encounter with the sea of judgmental eyes,
perpetually analyzing our worth, value, and purpose,
and then, finally, our wailing cry—the primal indication of our
rejection of a world so initially painful.

Strange then, how this suffering was at once alleviated
when placed into the two arms of our loving mother.

In this moment, we looked upward to
behold our first moment of beauty,
our first affirmation of life.

WREATH OF ROSE THORNS

I want to be the
type of person
whose mere being
alleviates the
suffering of others.

LITTLE ABSURD WORLD

Live your life in
constant amazement
at how wonderfully
absurd it all is.

THINGNESS

The moment I awaken
from my night of deep rest
and my consciousness
emerges from out of its depths,
I experience something peculiar—
I remember that *I am a thing*
and how absurd this fact is.

PARADOX

The deeper you think about death
the greater your fear grows,
until suddenly you reach a depth
where even fear no longer draws breath,
and then it dissolves.

DAS NICHTS

She had finally asked him,

"So then, tell me—what happens after you die?"

He gave a long, drawn-out sigh, as if to express
the many years he had toiled over this question—
years of sweat,
of blood,
of torment.
He then replied, with somber eyes,

"Nothing."

When the creator extends his brush
into the world, he must do so with the
unshakable certainty that his brush is
not really a knife in disguise
slashing the world to pieces.

MISTAKES

And, my mistakes will end up
being the lessons I teach to others.

A SHIP'S HELM

Little did you know of the tether that
emanates from out of your breast—
invisible, and yet, pulling you,
through time, to an aim.

Freedom consists in
your taking hold of it,
becoming its navigating master.

BEHIND A BILLION STARS

Most poets revel in the stars.

But, let me become the type of poet
who peers into the murky
void between the stars,
to see what secrets lie there.

HISTORY OF
THE SAOL

PART II

HISTORY OF THE SAOL: PART II

As the guide continued his impromptu lecture on the history of the Saol, my eyes were caught within the beauty of the Matisse painting.

I wondered what it would feel like to be one of the pale-painted people depicted in the scene—so ostensibly red of heart, so unquestionably full of life. Looking back, I realize how much I had, at the time, envied the subjects within *Joy of Life*. But even so, I could not pull my gaze away—my eyes were stuck to the colours of the canvas.

Although I was gripped by the brilliant hues of Henri Matisse, I kept my ears attentive and listened carefully to the guide as he continued to talk of the origin of the Saol.

"The Master was a very rich man—one of exceptional wealth, even by today's standards. But, even with all this money at his disposal, he was perpetually unhappy, and nothing seemed to help. He would walk along the dark and wet streets of the city night, peering into the eyes of people who beamed with life, and could not, himself, understand why it was he who had been sentenced to suffer! Along those streets he roamed for days and nights, weeks and months, deep within a stream of tormented thought—even though he owned many cars, many houses, and innumerable possessions, having enough money at his fingertips that it would have been impossible to spend a mere fraction of it.

"However, this walking—it did nothing. This thinking—it did nothing. And so, he did as any reasonable person would do in a time of inner turmoil and expanded his horizons. First, he converted to Christianity. And for a fleeting moment, he felt a spark of life. However, the spark was present only when he walked into the most brilliantly constructed cathedrals around the world—the

Notre Dame de Paris, the Sistine Chapel in the Vatican City, Saint Basil's Cathedral in Russia, and Santa Maria del Fiore in Florence. Amhrán tells us that those were of the Master's favourite— that the Master would talk of their architecture with such profound reverence. But still, during this brief period of Christianity, his happiness always seemed *just* out of reach—that after he had left those magnificent cathedrals, he would, once again, feel unwelcomed by existence. He would feel *homeless*. He would feel *out of place*.

"So, he carved yet another path—in fact, this would be the start of a recurring pattern. He went through all the major Western religions, with Judaism and Islam to start. During these periods, he would again use his money and travel to the four corners of Earth to practice his newfound faith, within the most impressive buildings dedicated to each of the religions. He visited the Great Synagogue of Florence, the Jubilee Synagogue of Prague, the Szeged Synagogue of Hungary, then the Al-Masjid an-Nabawi Mosque of Saudi Arabia, and the Sultan Ahmed Mosque of Turkey. It is rumoured that he had even completed the Islamic pilgrimage to the Great Mosque of Mecca. During these moments, he felt the surging spark of life. But, still, when he returned home, his unhappiness followed—these sparks, he found, were fleeting feelings—and he knew Western religion was not his answer."

PRIMALITY

My stomach grumbled, and for a moment I could think of nothing
other than the primal desire to devour. The thought of lions tearing
at the throat of a helpless antelope flashed before my mind with
ferocious rapidity, and the image of I, in human form, naked on
all fours, striding beside the pack of lions in galloping leaps to
sink my teeth into warm fleshly food—blood blanketing my
mouth and dripping off my sharp animal canines—glossy and red,
glistening in the blaze of the African sun.

A
glorious
animalistic,
deterministic,
mechanistic,
existence.

CONVERSATION

We plant words on each other's
ears like little kisses in our verbal
foreplay. But fair warning—if
this debate heats up this way,
with your opinionated bites to
my neck, and my teeth marks of
controversy trailing below your
chest, soon we'll be possessed
by intercourse for the intellect.

OPPOSITION

Your freedom is revealed
when the choice you make
is difficult, because it involves
a *striving away* from allowing
the world to choose for you.

QUIETUDE

These brief moments
of quietude
for the chaotic and
creative mind
are simultaneously
relieving yet,
frightening.

Will the onslaught
of ideas return
once again?

LUMINOUS

Always strive to become
a flashing beacon of difference
within the darkened crowd of similarity!

THRESHOLD

Loving you
is the same feeling
as being confronted
with the sublimity
of the universe.

It is a
paradoxical dance
of uncertainty and
understanding.

SAND

The average person will live
for 27, 375 days.

Whether you think of this
as a small number or a large
number speaks volumes
to your character.

SWORD OF DAMOCLES

The weirdness of being human is
veiled behind the routine of being human.

While I ride the subway, I am greatly
astonished that everyone sits and quietly
awaits their stop—this *sitting* dangles,
only by the thread of regularity.

They are hopelessly unaware of the
absurdity that looms overhead!

AN ODE TO ALBERT

Death must close my book,
for I will never run out of
words to give the world!

CANVAS

The Greeks have their *Discobolus* of Myron and their *Venus de Milo*, and the Italians have their *David*. And we have our pylons—those inescapable orange-and-black cylindrical and cone-shaped obelisks littered throughout our cities.

The Greeks have their Parthenon, the Egyptians have their Great Sphinx of Giza, and the French have their Notre Dame de Paris. And we have our towering metal cranes disfiguring the blue of the sky.

With the arrival of spring and summer, comes the incessant droning of jackhammers crunching the concrete, the terrorizing vehicle beeps that elicit reflexive grimacing, and, not the least, the bellowing groans from the engines of loaders, excavators, and dump-trucks whose only escape exists within the auditory isolation of two tiny, white earbuds cranked to full blast.

But this is to be expected, given the modern aesthetic: *The Construction Zone.*

Our modern industrial society, with its emphasis on ceaseless development, has neglected beauty. In its place, we've erected construction zones as the predominant aesthetic—complete with sight and sound.

This comes at a grave cost to consciousness, which is nourished by its confrontations with *the beautiful*.

Many philosophers agree that suffering is an inextricable feature of human existence, which can in part be made bearable by the phenomenon of beauty.

So, I ask, where in our great cities are we to turn when we suffer?

No longer do our cities offer us refuge in the form of architectural wonder—those special monuments that show us the world is still good.

And even worse, when we now feel the weight of the world on our shoulders, we are enveloped within the intolerable clamouring of hacksaws and the discordant melody of moaning machinery. We are caught in a labyrinth of orange-chained fences that dictate our freedom of mobility. We have no choice but to endure infuriating traffic jams caused by an endless phalanx of neon-patterned pylons. And we are forced to traverse innumerable five-foot dirt-mound exhibits that, with even a frail gust of wind, obscures our vision of the world within a brown, murky visage.

When we are confronted by the suffering of day-to-day human life, our new aesthetic does not embrace us like the architecture of bygone eras; rather, it only adds fuel to our fiery anguish.

Consequently, our new aesthetic movement must be described as one of anti-art, of anti-beauty.

And so, I plead, hopefully alongside the passionate citizenry of the modern world that we work to change course and follow in the footsteps of our great artistic ancestors, remembering, in the words of Henry David Thoreau, that "this world is but canvas to our imaginations" (*A Week on the Concord and Merrimack Rivers,* 1849).

HISTORY OF
THE SAOL

PART III

"Amhrán tells us that the Master, determined to find *a way—a cure for his sickness,* then shifted his focus toward the religions of the East. He began with Buddhism and was especially drawn to the Buddhist truism that *life is suffering.* This strummed the deepest chord of his Being. '*Finally,*' he thought, '*others have come to the same conclusion!*' But the long, drawn-out hours of meditation seemed like a complete renunciation of life! That during these long meditative hours, he found himself face-to-face with what ailed him most—*his unhappiness.*

"Then, he did what he had always done. He used his money to travel to the greatest Buddhist temples and monasteries the world had to offer—the Wat Arun Buddhist temple of Bangkok, the Yonghe Temple of China, and the Paro Taktsang Monastery of Bhutan. And, once again, there were sparks of life; yet, this was only when he was found within the temples and monasteries. After he had left for home, his unhappiness followed."

———— ⋙⋘ ————

It was during a university-funded trip abroad that I came across this strange and wondrous group of people.

My first-year anthropology professor described the Saol as a 'remote and isolated cult with a peculiar set of belief structures, perfect for the academically curious,' although my choice to sojourn overseas was not guided by any insatiable curiosity.

No, it was decidedly an attempt to distance myself from a home I had perceived as being devoid of promise.

This sojourn was a hastened escape. And my sudden departure from home was without any reason other than an effort to drown out the incessant inner chatter of my own feelings of dejection and purposelessness, feelings I had mistakenly attributed to my place of upbringing...

ID

I am a demon!
But, that is why I am
so goddamn interesting
to angels.

ABUNDANT

I am so happy that
it feels *weird; wrong* even—
as if I have fortuitously tapped into
a restricted well of abundance
that the rest of the world has
rejected, as if the communal
consensus posits that people are
not supposed to be *this* happy,
and at every moment,
I can't help but defy
this unspoken precept.

GOYA'S SATURN

Each wrist and ankle is bound by
familiar shackles that keep you
imprisoned in the cell of ego.

Heavy is the chain of resentment,
the chain of pride,
the chain of insecurity,
and the chain of apathy,
weighing down your arms
and legs to inactivity.

The heaviest of chains grip at
your neck with the strength of a
million hands—*fear.*

The key has always rested in
between your index and thumb,
and the frailty of the precarious
prison will *only* collapse
under the pressure of
your most potent power:
human freedom.

NIRVANA OR SUICIDE

Nihilism, and Buddhist
conceptions of enlightenment
are at bottom the same thing.

And while the former manifests
as resentment and the latter as empathy,
their goal is ultimately the same—
the dissolution of the value of the self.

CAFFEINE

Coffee makes the absurdity
of the world bearable.

CAVALRY

No more meaningless conversation.

You must declare war on my mind.
Lay siege to this fortified neurological
citadel. Surround it with the mightiest
phalanx of ideas and dethrone these
dogmatic kings who have grown too
comfortable in their position of power
over the kingdom of my brain.

PLUCKED WINGS

What we lose in a mass society
is what is divine within each person,
replacing this divinity with
horrid dispensability.

Such is the case being fallen angels
with tags that say *replaceable.*

COMPASS

Every writer should have a
goal to guide their pen and ink.

My goal is to satirize reality
itself, revealing all of its mistakes.

ROT

My eyelids droop to slits, as my spirit drifts away. Yet, my limbs are caught in algorithmic hypnosis, continuing to fold the messy and mountainous mass of dress shirts left from the previous night. I am paid minimum wage to be an algorithm.

> *Function: remove the hanger from underneath the dress shirt and throw the hanger into the cardboard box to my side.*
> *Function: button the dress shirt to the top.*

The boredom is really kicking in today.

> *Function: place the shirt on the table with the back of the shirt facing upward.*
> *Function: fold the shirt in perfect angles.*

Is there a way to live with the boredom without striving to escape it? Is this what our striving really consists in—a mere *striving away* from boredom? Does it not move us toward something better?

> *Function: place the folded dress shirt neatly to the side.*
> *Function: repeat.*

The boredom grips my neck with its sluggish fingers of monotony, and my striving lies in peeling away each finger, one at a time. You think you chase after something in order to achieve some higher tier of life? No, you chase after something because the chase quells the boredom that would otherwise drive you completely mad.

OMNISCIENCE REQUIRED

I have been the religious.
I have been the philosopher.
I have been the student, the lover, the trickster.

I ask: *What is it that is constant in these roles other than a fear
of committing to one?*

Truly, am I not a mere multiplicity?

I have been the disgruntled employee triumphantly quitting his
job. I have been the iconoclast, reducing cherished beliefs to ash.
I have been the seducer, the boyfriend, and Zarathustra as well.

I am contradiction, and yet, I am unperturbed.

It is rational fear that conditions my avoidance of choosing a
prevailing identity—a rational fear that develops after the bloody
death of God.

These identities act as different guiding principles as I traverse
the oppressive infinity that each moment presents.

To *choose an identity* is the greatest commitment—and I revile
it. Instead, let me jump from one identity to the next, like Albert
Camus' actor, only the stage set before me is the world and the
audience is but one—*a barren universe who peers back, with the
glossy eyes of the abyss.*

Every day, I witness the choices people make.
How can you bear the burden and choose?

Here is a fact: *A human is simply not capable of choosing the optimal choice in every given moment for the whole of his life!*

In fact, I'm unconvinced that humans have ever made the optimal choice, except by the hands of mere chance.

I am unconvinced not because I am a cynic nor a misanthrope—quite the opposite. Rather, it is because of the dizzying number of possible choices that are presented with each dawning moment.

Ask yourself: *Can any human analyze an infinity in a mere instant?*

Truly, let me remain a multiplicity.

HISTORY OF
THE SAOL

PART IV

HISTORY OF THE SAOL: PART IV

My guide continued speaking of the Master.

"This pattern of religious conversion had persisted for years. He converted to Hinduism, Jainism, Taoism, and all the different sects of Christianity. He converted to many of the smaller, newer religions as well as new age philosophies that practiced 'presence' associated with the dissolution of one's ego. But, the outcome remained the same, and he continued to feel overwhelmingly dejected; he continued to feel a crippling sense of despair. He had lost hope and felt that the only fact that had become painfully clear to him, the only fact that reverberated through the heart of all religions, was that *life was suffering*. It was his inescapable truth."

The trip to the compound was grueling. It was a twenty-one-hour flight with two stopovers. That is not to mention the four-hour drive from the airport that brought me and two other weary travellers into the heart of the compound.

However, this afforded me the time to write, which had become an emotional oasis for me. All my thoughts would pour out onto paper. And then they would be there, on the page written in ink—instead of in here, within my mind, taking the form of inarticulate demons wreaking neurological havoc...

VANISH

Success should not be measured
by the gluttonous accumulation
of material wealth. Rather, it should
be measured by how happy and content
one would be given the *disappearance*
of all their possessions.

GNASHING DRAGON

Change your
response to fear
from avoidance
to confrontation.
In doing so,
you change
fear itself
into courage.

RA

Trees, grass, cars, people, or
signposts; things always
seem more real when it is
the sun that reveals them.

It is as if things were meant
to be seen in pure sunlight.

TO MOM, OUR HALCYON

It was a bright and sunny May afternoon.

The fragrance of freshly cut fields subtly lingered, dancing its
way into our noses, refreshing our senses after the long winter
months, and the warmth of the sun hugged our skin with an
infinity of outstretched rays.

Thinking back to this special day, I couldn't have been more
than four or five years old.

We were waiting outside of an elementary school—the name of
which has always slipped my mind—and there were fifteen
minutes to spare before the buzz of the bell—the buzz that
would signal the imminent rush of kids swarming in droves to
catch your school bus.

But, we had those glorious fifteen minutes, and they were spent
wisely.

We raced through the green of the school field to the distant
playground, far enough for the sight of the bus to recede into a
small speck in the distance.

The blue of the sky smiling down upon us, the warmth of May
encouraging us.

I laughed my way to the sizzling stones of the playground, *and
the world was good.*

I think of this moment as a turning point.

A realization that life is precious.

It is a memory I cherish, not simply because you are in it, but because it taught me that life is inextricably beautiful.

It was my first conscious confrontation with beauty, and it will forever be written along the crest of my heart.

So, thank you, for a memory I will never forget.

SONG

No music to feed
two famished ears,
is a baroque-painted universe
where eyes have disappeared.

BONE

Every single one of us
is a future skull.

ANIMAL, MAN, GOD

Within us exists the
unrivaled power that
has forever birthed
Gods from men:

*That our destiny rests
inside the palms of our
own radically free hands.*

However, dread has
convinced us that this
power is merely illusion.

A fear potent enough to
turn us into animals again.

REYNARD THE FOX

When our inner trickster beckons,
he will not be silenced, until he has been
satiated with belligerence and mischief.

Do not dare deny him.

MODERN MAN

Much of our life consists of chasing after a
definition of success unwittingly thrust upon us
by the education system.

A definition of success that, to our detriment,
solely focuses on *external* wealth.

It is no wonder that modern man
suffers from great *internal* poverty.

PRISON

Scabbed ankles drip blood down to the cell floor, a crimson silhouette traces the perimeter of each shackled foot. Catatonic you sit, fixated on keys jutting out the lock, as blood drops maneuver sweat and hair follicle obstacles. Liberation hangs onto cold, indifferent air, whirling 'round a phalanx of decrepit bodies—but you'd rather stay clung to the Decaying Negativity who melts into cracking concrete perpendiculars to your right. His pale, seeping skin adhering to the structure, becoming it. And your shitty excuse to stay chained by rusted metal to dying men, *"He reminds me of me!"*

But, the Decaying is without the crimson left to bloom—a glimpse at your own approaching depletion. His heart a shrivelled rose with the stench of corruption that pumped blush red to pores long ago. Now, only a peeling watercolour of uniform red swathed the cement—left as evidence of a once beating chest, defeated by willing ignorance of free will.

He too, shackled to a Negativity—a pile of porcelains—bony and broken at the ankle—a final self-inflicted fracturing of an illusory determinism, culminating with a triumphant, *"I'm free!"* but chose the frigid imprisonment with convincing whispers from the Decaying tongue crying, *"Please, don't leave me."*

What's left beside the two men—a scattered puzzle of a skeleton, flagrant in its display of entropy. The bony mass patiently awaits the fateful, fatal flame spit out a thrower gripped by ten dendritic fingers of the Positive to negate any evidence of the Negative's existence, except a reduced ash plume dancing idle in air. A merciless genocide conditioned by a conscious mind repeating the line, *"No more negative thoughts, no more negative thoughts."*

HISTORY OF THE SAOL

PART V

HISTORY OF THE SAOL: PART V

"The day finally arrived when the Master would have no more of this unhappiness and had decided that the only option that remained was to take his own life. He had come to the same justification that the *sick* people of today come to—that the unavoidable condition of human life was to suffer, and that the only way to end the suffering was to destroy the very conduit whereby suffering manifests—to destroy the thing that suffering lives within. Yes, *to destroy oneself.*"

———————

When I arrived at the compound, I was struck by its sheer magnitude.

It is said that the colony repurposed an old, abandoned university campus—purchased in full by the wealth of the Master.

There were magnificent pieces of artwork littered around the compound. I beheld both paintings and sculptures—original masterworks that were of artistic styles the Western world has never seen.

One marble sculpture in particular had struck me with visceral force. It stood in the centre of the main garden to the left of a tall, twisting willow tree. It was of a figure that resembled a Picasso painting come to life—utterly primal and disfigured. I wondered how many of the sick had stared into the contorted eyes of this disfigured face, transfixed and horrified at how perfectly the artist had depicted the image cast in their mirrors, transfixed and horrified at the familiarity of the marble face, a face that took on their own hopeless features.

REJECTED CASKET

My intrinsic motivation
is to produce such
beauty with such fervor
so as to transcend the
graveyard that I'll
inevitably lie in.

GLUTTON

There is nothing I am more
gluttonous for than words—
overindulging in books
to a degree unhealthy,
drinking up my time
with tales for the mind
until I am drunk off the
lives of others!

ZARATHUSTRA'S MUG

Nietzsche on the left,
coffee on the right,
Chopin against two eardrums,
while words acquaint each eye.

Immortality would be all right,
if I could do this, on repeat,
until the end of time.

DARING DISSENT

Be *daring*;
for every courageous
action is a revolution
against fear.

HANDS UPON A FACE OF DREAD

The dread of having the destiny
of your whole life at the tips
of your fingers can transform
even the steadiest of hands
into a trembling mess.

MUSE

It turns out that my muse
is a bustling Starbucks—
mere moments spent
within, and one is exposed
to the entirety of human behaviour.

ORDER! CHAOS!

Inside each of our heads
exists a bloodied battlefield
of kings and jesters.

Be wary of the
side that triumphs,
for the prevailing side,
will consume your mind
with either order or chaos!

WRITER'S BLOCK

These fingers betray me
for yesterday,
each typed away,
ablaze with the spirit
of Renaissance painters.

I am betrayed
by ten tiny
autonomous appendages,
who today,
commit the deadly
sin of sloth;
each finger weighing over
a thousand tonnes
rendering the production
of a mere thought
possible only at the hands
of an omnipotent God.

21ST CENTURY CONFLATION

Do not confuse sex with love.
They are subtly different phenomena.

There is a reason why casual sex
exists, but casual love doesn't.

SCYLLA AND CHARYBDIS

The background murmur of the clamouring customer is always present.

The gaze they shoot toward me is one of expected obligation—it speaks, *"You are here to fulfill my needs; it is of my needs that guide your action."*

I quickly avert my eyes. Though, not from insecurity. It is from a desire to remain free and undetermined in the face of subtle tyranny.

I scurry to the back room—a claustrophobic refuge, littered with towering boxes of various shoes, a thick layer of permeating dust, and a sticky taste of cardboard. Decidedly, I have sacrificed environmental comfort for the existential kind.

Back there, I am me. I am not their mechanism.

Every so often, I am summoned to the front desk, where people have lined up to determine me.

The oncoming and increasing murmur terrorizes my auditory pathways with discordant melody.

The beeps and rings and crashing objects, the rustling bags, and the loud crack of the stapler—the incessant *ring, ring, ringing* phone that I never pick up, the slamming of cupboards and drawers, the piercing cry of the baby, and worst of all the overbearing voice of customers shrieking their demands.

These are the drums of modern torment, increasing its tempo with each shift I take on; all the while, I am constantly aware of the malevolent stare of the clock, as it mocks me, laughing and pointing with two taunting hands.

It drags and drags and drags—the slow passage of time.

Each infinitesimal moment stretching out into a perceptible torture.

This, I endure—truly, without a why.

HISTORY OF
THE SAOL

PART VI

"The day the Master was set to take his own life, he sent for his servant to retrieve the required materials. In an effort to remain inconspicuous, the Master sent for a long list of items that were unrelated to the definitive act. He sent for a new black suit fitting his specific dimensions, several items from the grocer, and a few other items of an innocuous nature. However, he had also sent for a long, thick and twisted polypropylene rope with enough length necessary for the knot of a noose. The Master's servant unwittingly abided.

"However, after noticing that the Master—ignoring the other items—took the rope into his lodgings, after looking at it with the longing eyes of a man of great sorrow, the servant quickly grew privy to the state of mind that the Master bore. The servant immediately realized the mistake he had made in purchasing said rope, and in that moment, didn't know what to do."

I don't know what it was that I expected to find at the compound. I guess nothing of profound importance.

My departure from home wasn't a search for something more insightful—no, it was merely running away—running away from a life with no guiding principle and the inner harrowing that accompanied this purposelessness. It was a running away from the death of God, a running away from the dissolution of good and evil, a running away from nihilism. And not in the least, it was a running away from the suffering felt by every human. I left because of an overwhelming alienation from what it was that made people human—purpose, justification, and affirmation of life. Though, just like the Master, my unhappiness followed; these metaphysical constants followed. And, mere running was futile.

LORD OF FLIES

"Do I look good in this?" she asked.

He swivelled his chair around,
slowly looked her up and down,
and replied,

"You look good in everything,"
then smiled devilishly and said,
"and in nothing."

REVERIE

Mid-October breeze
splashing against a sea of
autumn-coloured leaves
is nature's sweet lullaby.

Midday nap
accompanied by a window crack
experiencing an irresistible
tranquilizing effect.

CHIMERAS

The mind is a prison
that we all mistake
for a home.

BUTTERFLY

Impassioned writers
must bloom
their cocooned
hearts into art.

ODE TO A BEST FRIEND

Best friendships
are conditioned
by a mutual reveling
in the absurd.

The friend is the
part of the world
that, to one, is
completely
understood:

That even though the
world turns its back,
the friend is that
who never would.

WISHING, STRIVING, WANTING, CRYING

These inanimate objects
stare at me with two
eyes of seething envy.

All wish to be able to wish.
All strive to be able to strive.
All want to be able to want,
and cry and love and die!

They hate me, for I take these
little gifts of consciousness
for granted, while they sit there
unable to have even one thought
manifested.

HOME

"So, when will you go home?"
she asked the enigmatic vagabond,
with profound puzzlement.

With unwavering conviction,
he replied,
"This horizon is my living room,
this brain is my lamp,
this heart is my book,
and this ocean is my coffee.
Only here can I flick on the light,
open to any page I like, and sip
upon the sublimity of life! I am home."

MELLIFLUOUS

A human life is remedied
by the dips and peaks of
soft melodies.

SLEEPING PENCILS

A writer's constant struggle:

Fight to resist
gravity's grip
on those sluggish lids
that droop to slits,
long enough
to call upon
the God's of the
lead-imbued stick.

ORCHID

A flower blooms, is beautiful, then dies—is this tragedy?

The nihilist would say so—he would say, *"Better off the flower never existed."* But to follow this train of thought to its bitter end, is to condemn the whole of existence, and wish for it to have never been!

Instead, let our response be to partake in beauty's mere moment, even with an eternity of entailed destruction.

ROULETTE

An indiscriminate universe
dishes fortune or catastrophe,
with an abyss for eyes, utterly blind
to its consequence on our lives.

PARABOLA

The walls are closing in!

"Why believe in God without any evidence?"

These walls, they're tall and formidable!

"The argument from evil is of such logical coherence. If God exists, as well as evil—which it does—then God is either malevolent and all-powerful, or he lacks power."

I cannot see past them!

"Who has seen God? Where exactly is He? If God exists, then why doesn't He make himself known?"

The walls are in every direction! I run through any passage I find but a thousand bricks immediately erupt from the ground below, erecting themselves around me. They form walls that are imposing, and of impenetrable fortitude. Each wall towers toward the sky until it obscures the horizon, and its height dissolves the clouds above.

I see a glimmer of light at the corner of my eye.

I sprint toward it with hope and determination.

But, the glint is elusive and ultimately an illusion—a mere remnant of a past scaffold.

"If God created me, then He also created me without the capacity to believe in Him, and if believing in Him is the path to

*heaven, and furthermore, that disbelief is condemnable to an
eternity in hell, how is that just?"*

I find myself caught in a labyrinthine jungle of confusing walls,
and I make them my home because escape is impossible. I have
become accepting of them, without noticing that their roots seep
through the skin of Earth, corrupting me from the depths below.

*"How is it that I have a justice system that is more complex and
logical than God Himself?"*

I am muddied by the logic of it all, dazed by their height, by
their opacity. They are the skyscrapers of hyper-rationalism that
scratch at the blue of the sky until it peels back, revealing the
glossy, black abyss behind. I am left staring up at a deepened
cavity swallowing consciousness whole.

They grow taller and taller, and I spiral further and further.

God is now a distant speck and to make out His figure requires a
squint of unprecedented strain. He cannot be resurrected.

I have lost my way and have begun to add bricks to my own
demise.

And now the walls have towered so tall they have arched into a
parabolic dome. Under which, I am stranded, in the heart of its
barren centre with nothing to do but analyze its structure and
conclude that the walls are necessary.

HISTORY OF
THE SAOL

PART VII

HISTORY OF THE SAOL: PART VII

"But, it suddenly occurred to the servant that he might have a plan after all, one that might work to save the Master from suicide. All at once, he had remembered that at the beginning of his employment, his Master had frequented the museum, always returning with that spark of life. He thought to himself that whatever it was at the museum would surely be what was needed to stop the Master from taking his own life. At the very least, it would rouse the Master with some interest—one that would afford the servant some time to devise a more thorough strategy. This was a shot in the dark, but there was nothing else.

"With a little guile, but not without some resistance on the part of the Master, the servant managed to convince the Master to take him to the museum—the Master was a kind-hearted man, even though he was severely black of heart, and he enjoyed bringing his servants to places they could never afford to go on their own dime. And so, there they stood—the Master and servant—staring at the original painting, *Joy of Life* by Henri Matisse. At first, neither spoke a word. The Master stared at the painting with blank expression, while the servant was filled with great concern for the man he had worked alongside for many years. The Master turned to the servant with a simple, *'Thank you.'* The servant had no idea what to make of it—or if this trip to the museum would have any effect on him. That night, the servant tossed and turned, unable to fall asleep—knowing that by sunrise he might walk in on a Master no more."

During my stay, I conversed with many of the Saol people.

Through these long conversations, I had become painfully aware of the difference between the Saol and myself.

They had a principle, a value—a firm scaffold at the bottom of their Being that held their actions high with justification—and I did not.

All I had was a pad and a pen—but my writings reflected a preoccupation with death, meaninglessness, and human suffering...

CREATIVE CORPUS

I see human art and creation as the spirit that guides each set of eyes toward the spiraling staircase leading to the ancient oak lever at the heart of Earth's fiery core—the lever of the question of Being, the lever of the question of Time. Human creativity is the collective spirit that calls upon the blue hearts of consciousness and pleads for their participation in the great questions of life!

I thus devote myself to humanity's creative corpus.

My work inevitable and undying while I breathe and beat the drums of biology—joining hands with the great ethos of our species, but not in a "victorious and illusory cry of the blinded artist [who says]: 'I have said everything,' but [in my death] which closes [my] experience and the book of [my Being]," as the great Albert Camus once said (*The Myth of Sisyphus*, 1942).

STRANGENESS

The sheer
strangeness
of being
human is
cloaked
behind a
veil of
routine.

COGNAC

A philosopher once told me
as I winced from a shot of chaos,

"It's okay friend, none of
us truly get used to it."

RED

When you
are consumed
by rage, it is
your body's
way of saying:

"Pay attention to what
you want to do next,
for it is a glimpse into
the darkest corners of
what you are capable of."

TO DAD, OUR HALCYON

You want to go fishing?
Sure, when?
Now.

Reese's peanut butter cups, salted Lay's chips, six frosty Cokes—cans, not the bottles, because Coke in a can tastes better—Mars bars, Flaming Hot Cheetos, a slab of salami, a brick of cheddar, the list goes on. "Buy whatever you want," you said. "You're an adult today." We bought the whole damn convenience store, stuffing it into our shitty little pine-green dodge caravan, and in an instant, we were headed off to Snakeskin Lake.

Only fifteen minutes prior had we loaded the van's trunk with tackle galore—my shiny, new tackle box leaning against your heavily weathered one, a cylindrical tube stocked with lightweight fishing rods—ones that could be bent into a complete circle, which made the fight all the more glorious—two reels that had been fed with fishing line earlier in the summer, hooks, bobbers, sinkers, needle-nose pliers, plastic worms we never used, and not in the least, our favourite lure—*the dying flutter.*

The two-and-a-half-hour trip to Parry Sound was not put to waste, with a well lectured crash course on classic music from the sixties, and captivating stories of your Yorkville hippie days. I distinctly remember listening to "House of the Rising Sun" by The Animals—the guitar's dark melody, the clattering hi-hats, the wild synth piano keys, and Eric Burdon's voice as he passionately sung about a gambling man—these instruments will forever resound in my head, reminding me of this fishing trip.

After maneuvering our van atop a winding road through a thick plume of forestry, we finally arrived at our destination—

Snakeskin Lake—of course, with half our snacks already devoured. Snakeskin Lake itself was a long, narrow, and winding body of water, but it was teeming with smallmouth bass—our lurking opponent.

From out of some camouflaging shrubbery, you extracted your little metal boat, and we pushed it into the lake—but not before attaching the boat's engine and loading it with our food and tackle for the day.

There is no better feeling in the world than cruising along the waters of Northern Ontario in a shabby boat, feeling the cold water splashing against and soothing an already sunburnt face from the unrelenting rays of an August sun.

Ten minutes later, we had found the perfect spot for smallmouth bass—a shallow feeding spot at the threshold of the lake and the shore. With our dying flutters tied tight to our line, we whipped our rods and cast, sending the lure flying toward the green lily pads. The distinctive whistling of the reel letting go of fishing line and the *plunk* of the dying flutter meeting the surface of the water meant that the time had come for a father and his son to wait for the fight they had longed for in the sweltering heat of their van—namely, a hungry bass pitted against the joy of a kid fishing alongside his old man.

You want to go fishing?
Sure, when?
Now.

SOCRATES

There is a subtle
pleasure in making
happy people happier
and mad people madder.

DEATH OF OBJECTIVITY

She finally asked me,
"Is life better than death?"

"The truth is irrelevant," I replied.
*"What matters is that you live
your life as if the answer to that
question is a resounding yes!"*

A LIFE UNLIVED

Passion pleads our
freedom to tear off
the chains of an
unlived life.

INNER WORK

Most never take the time
to tend their world within.

How common it has become
to encounter a mind terrorized
by storms and floods of unimaginable
ferocity—to witness a once utopian
mind drown under rising tides.

SISYPHUS SMILE

Today, I awoke with an
uncontainable smile
conditioned by a
cup overflowing
with purpose.

I am
reminded
by this existential
grin that I am of infinite
value.

HISTORY OF
THE SAOL

PART VIII

"The sun arose, and the servant was surprised and relieved to see that the Master had awoken with it. The Master sat at the kitchen table, sipping upon a cup of coffee with a subtle smile and said, *'I wish to go back to the museum with you tonight.'* And so, they did—and they did so for many subsequent weeks, establishing a new recurring pattern.

"During those visits, the both of them would stand in front of *Joy of Life*, staring with great intensity. Over the course of those weeks, the servant had become less concerned about the mental well-being of the Master and had himself started to appreciate the work of art set before him."

———————

The Saol people have strange mannerisms and traditions. None that I have ever seen performed in Western culture.

Once a month, they have festivals of appreciation that are dedicated to the phenomenon of beauty. Unfortunately, the timing of my visit did not permit me to partake in one of these appreciative festivals, but I hear that one of their main attractions are the life-sized re-enactments of famous paintings that allow the Saol people to walk through the landscapes of Picasso, Matisse, and Van Gogh—to live for a moment what they have marvelled at for a lifetime.

Another peculiarity of the Saol way of life is their birth painting ceremony. Every time a baby is birthed, the baby is passed around the Saol people, who mark the crying newborn with a smear of coloured paint. By the end of the ceremony, the baby is a rainbow of acrylic. My guide told me that this ceremony represents the colony's attempt to combat the child's first moment of suffering—who enters the unfamiliar world, crying and gasping for air—with a moment of communal beauty. That the first thing that must be taught to the baby—if only unconsciously—is to combat suffering by becoming a canvas...

ELECTRIC ZEUS

I am Immanuel Kant.
I am Rodion Raskolnikov.
I am Reynard the Fox.

Yet, I am none of these.

I am crucified Christ.
I am great Gilgamesh.
I am electric Zeus.

Yet, I am none of these.

I am Dionysus and Apollo.
I am you.
I am the past, present, and future.

Yet, I am none of these.

I am the sum total of the thoughts of all people who are, them-selves, the sum total of the thoughts of those who had come before them.

I wonder if, one day, I will conjure a thought of my own.

I wonder if, one day, I will create something the world has yet to see.

I wonder if, one day, I will cease being the mouthpiece for what has already been said.

I am Carl Gustav Jung when I say that ideas have taken hold of me, and I have yet to take hold of them.

A MESSAGE TO THE WORLD

Break open your ribcage
and behold the bone shards that
crash against the skin of the Earth!

Reach deep within and clench your
bleeding, beating heart and present
it as sacrifice to the thing you
love most.

Life pleads for this kind of
passion from people—*bloody
and sacrificial passion.*

LUXURIA

"I am in love with her."

But, he was unaware of the
parasitic deviant infesting
the streets of his brain—
Lust they called it.

It prowled this neural metropolis,
vandalizing the clean brick walls
of every street, alley, and pathway
with empty '*I love yous*' until his
brain was swathed in unrequited
romantic appetite.

What he called,
"Love at first sight."

INVIDIA

The reaper arrives
with hands that
grip a scythe
to collect the minds
of those dwindling
in life.

Sent as an emissary
of the most envious entity;
The Void, Nothing, and Empty,
The Loather of Existence,
wanting nothing more than
to drag Being into
pale oblivion.

GULA

The Seducer's Mantra:

I am gluttonous
for your love, it's just,
I am also hungry for hers;
this is the difficulty in being
a Napoleon of Hearts!

To conquer, only to
want the '*next her*'—
this is my life's lot;
this will dictate,
indefinitely,
driven by
intoxicated
new love.

VANAGLORIA

Instagram:

The narcotic of choice
for the insatiably vain;
that small percentage
who define inner value
by the number of likes
to their name.

AVARICE

Dead is the man who
hoarded only knowledge
that's written,
killed at the hands
of ignoring the
obvious truism:

That it takes one part
written knowledge
mixed with equal parts
experience to properly
execute the recipe
for worldly wisdom.

IRA

His mouth twitching and rabid,
eyes deranged and pushed to paint,
splashing red against
the helpless victim of his rage!

It was a wrathful Tour de Force.

Red paint splattering the canvas.
Each brush stroke was a
shrieking yell of madness,
or a jab he could
never reel back in.

The final touch of his
masterpiece of wrath was
a frenzied fist,
to culminate
with a bloodied face
that would permanently
destroy a friendship.

IRA PART II

Do not let your wrath
turn you whistling-kettle mad
at irrelevant slights
to bypass.

ACEDIA

You've laid your love for me
with the slothful.

I colour it with the nostalgic
hues of our past love—saturated
with effort and attempt.

It is only a matter of time now,
before my love grows slothful too.

And then, we'll know
why they call it a
deadly sin.

GAME OF CHILDREN

The world is a more nuanced
and complex iteration of a
playground.

We all play a game.
There are winners and losers.
And, every so often, someone
falls down, gets hurt,
and the game stops.

Only then, do we witness a true
glimpse into what is beautiful and ugly
about human existence.

PUPPETEER

Make sure you are not
passively allowing your
choices to be made by
factors other than your own
inner conscious arbiter.

Burst forth your freedom!

ANT FARM

I sit here, on my break in the mall and eat a crumbly and shitty café cookie, two eyes consciously slouched to blurs.

I observe a sea of people, endlessly drifting by—wave after wave of mirrored copies.

The clamour of their indistinct sound hugs me for too long turning me irritably claustrophobic.

Their tether moves them from store to store unaware that they search for something more than mere product. The hope is that their purchase will drown out their inner feeling of meaninglessness—and so, they trudge on in search of what will satiate this need, if only to be fed for a brief and dwindling moment, a moment that will *poof* into a little plume of dust, with the soft touch of ten trembling fingers.

What is your aim? You have to be able to articulate what you move toward and why. If not, you are utterly lost. If not, the swallowing cement of comfortability will take hold and you will live out your dying days drifting the endless labyrinth of storefronts drawn in by their neon glare and fluorescent warmth.

But, the hug they offer is frigid, and their embrace is an empty promise of existential fortitude.

HISTORY OF
THE SAOL

PART IX

"Now, on one particular warm, summer night, the Master and servant set off to the museum. The servant's previous concern had returned as they drove, looking over at his Master, who was by this point, uncharacteristically pensive and withdrawn—as if the Master's mental progress had suddenly relapsed. That night, they stood in front of *Joy of Life* for an unusually long period of time— the Master had not moved a muscle nor had his eyes wavered— his eyes fixated on the two passionate kissers in the foreground, the carefree clarinet musician in the middle, and the reds and teals and swirling watercolours dancing upon the canvas. This intense fixation carried on for more than an hour. Then suddenly, to the surprise of the servant, his Master burst out in ecstasy, exclaiming, *'I have the answer! The problem is impotent!'*

"That night, they went home, and the Master dictated a series of epiphanies—ones that he had had over the course of those weeks staring intently at *Joy of Life*—the servant feverishly wrote them down."

What follows are the Master's nine epiphanies—the epiphanies that now serve to condition the Saol people. Each of which will be demarcated with a dove.

THE TEST

The depth of your spirit
is not revealed by how
calm you remain while
meditating, but by how
calm you remain in the
face of great adversity.

A HARROWING MIRACLE

Love is what keeps most
eyes peeled in the nighttime.

But, my eyes are stirred
by the fact that I am a mere property
of the thirty-seven trillion cells that make up
my body—a fact both incredible,
and yet, incomparably terrifying.

QUILL

To be a writer is to
develop the capacity
to see experiences
as potential art.

MAGNET

There is nothing sexier
than a person who is
unrelenting in their
passionate pursuit
of purpose.

TORRENTIAL TICK-TOCK

With each tick of the clock,
a letter,
a word,
a sentence
escaped.

With each tock of the clock,
a trillion photons crashed against
his screen-illuminated face,
until his idea manifested
within a torrent of verbal
aesthetic perfection.

HISTORY OF THE SAOL

THE FIRST EPIPHANY

HISTORY OF THE SAOL: THE FIRST EPIPHANY

The first of such epiphanies is that the truism shared by the world religions, which states that *life is suffering* is not *only* to be construed as an inextricable feature of human existence but also as the fundamental obstacle to be overcome by the very way we live our life—by the very way we choose to manifest our Being.

That, the correct response to human suffering is not a mere *passive* acceptance of the phenomenon, but rather, an *active* acceptance. Namely, a constant striving to reduce it, squash it, level it, and in a few words: *to justify it!*

And, it is by way of justifying of our lives as suffering beings that a transcendence of suffering can be achieved.

PURGATORIO

Those souls adrift
in purgatory must endure
a subway commute that
is spanned toward infinity.

Travelling by subway
from point A to B
replaces twenty minutes
of your life with a
meaningless waiting—
the same punishment
thrust upon those souls
found within the
pale oblivion.

Objects have more life in them
then we tend to give them credit for.

The object completely devoid of life
would be imperceptible to the
human eye.

COUP D'ÉTAT

The most glorious
coup d'état:

When the words 'I will'
overthrow the words
'I should.'

IDYLLIC PRESCRIPTION

An afternoon
walk through
an autumn
forest is the
most underrated
medication.

TRICKSTER

One of life's practical jokes:

We begin our life rich in time
but with impoverished minds.

We finish our life
developed in mind
but with zero time.

HISTORY OF
THE SAOL

THE SECOND EPIPHANY

HISTORY OF THE SAOL: THE SECOND EPIPHANY

The second of such epiphanies is that it is through *the beautiful* that we make strides to overcome suffering—with aesthetic judgments being another inextricable feature of human existence.

It is when beauty penetrates through the barrier of our suffering that we are able to transcend our condition as suffering beings for a fleeting moment!

This *transcendence* is the moment whereby we become *accepting* of our condition as suffering beings, the moment whereby we happily bear our suffering in exchange for life!

COLD PILLOW

Of all the Casanovas,
and all the Cleopatras,
there is still nothing
to exist, with a more
seductive grip than the
embrace of my bed while
I'm falling asleep.

SYMPOSIUM

One friend
masterful at
conversation
is worth more
than a million
friends who are
not.

LOTHARIO'S CUBE

Put away the Sudoku's,
puzzles, and Rubik's
cubes, and pick up a
woman's mind, the
most intricate puzzle,
the most satisfying
brain teaser.

Follower quantity does not
determine inner quality.

DANCE OF DASEIN

Each one of us
is a dancer
in the great
choreography
of Being and Time.

HISTORY OF THE SAOL

THE THIRD EPIPHANY

HISTORY OF THE SAOL: THE THIRD EPIPHANY

The third of such epiphanies is that the definition of *the beautiful* is that within the world, which when judged aesthetically, *tilts* your answer to the moral question of ontology— *'Is Being better than Nothing?'*—toward the positive, toward the *'Yes!'*

And, the definition of *the ugly* is that within the world, which when judged aesthetically, *tilts* your answer to the moral question of ontology toward the negative, toward the *'No!'*

The former is a *transcendence of suffering*—the moment whereby we become accepting of our condition as suffering beings—while the latter is a *succumbing to suffering*—the moment whereby we become rejecting of our condition as suffering beings.

These two phenomena—namely, aesthetic experience (i.e. beauty, ugly, and our judgments) and the proclamation of either the *'Yes!'* or the *'No!'*—are experienced simultaneously.

We are *confronted* with what is beautiful or what is ugly, not of our own volition, but rather as an aesthetic *gripping*, and it is precisely at the moment of being aesthetically *gripped*, that we proclaim the *'Yes!'* or the *'No!'* respectively.

They are simultaneous in the order of occurring events because the proclaimed answers *require* the beautiful or the ugly as sufficient *justification* for acceptance or rejection. The *'Yes!'* and the *'No!'* must have this metaphysical grounding. For example, we are aesthetically gripped by beauty, which in turn allows us to transcend the weight of our suffering through an instinctive, immediate, and wordless understanding that at the threshold of the interaction between human experience and the external world exists *something*, which justifies our condition as *suffering beings*. This something is beauty, and this understanding consists in both a recognition that we are not *only* suffering beings, but that we are also *beauty perceiving beings*—and that *life is worth its suffering just for these experienced moments of profound beauty*. This is the pre-rational justification that metaphysically grounds us in the *'Yes!'*

And so, that is precisely how this *tilting* works—the beautiful is that within the world, which when judged aesthetically provides us with a pre-rational justification for why life is worth living despite the suffering that life entails. *Experiences of beauty affirm a life of suffering, through an instinctive and immediate claim to accept suffering in exchange for aesthetically gripping moments of beauty*—it is precisely in these moments that the *'Yes!'* is proclaimed as the answer to the moral question of ontology—the tilt toward life.

Conversely, the ugly is that within the world, which when judged aesthetically reduces our justification to bear human suffering. *Experiences of the ugly deny a suffering life, through an instinctive and immediate claim to reject suffering in light of the aesthetically gripping moments that ugliness presents*—it is precisely in these moments that the *'No!'* is proclaimed as the answer to the moral question of ontology, or alternatively, it is that which conditions us with the pre-rational justification for suicide and destruction—the tilt toward death.

VULTURE OVERHEAD

Be wary of those who always
ask for advice but never take heed.

They are the savage scavengers
of solution, picking at your
carcass with their sharpened
beaks of worry and trouble,
until you are stripped clean
of all meat.

Never satiated, they always
move on in search of another
carcass to feed upon.

FLUTE

"How have you
turned your life around so successfully?"

"I became a snake charmer and hypnotized
the venomous serpents that had burrowed their
dwelling within my psyche."

A KING'S QUEEN

"Why must you write
so obsessively?"

"Because a written word is
more permanent than a thought,
and a book is more permanent
than consciousness. It is
the only way to stalemate
Death in his game of chess."

NAYSAYER

With each negative person
you surround yourself with,
a new cell bar is erected.

Select those you let into your
life with utmost caution, as
you may inadvertently construct
your own imprisonment!

NICOTINE

You seize a mere
portion of their screen,
so craft your words
carefully,
and learn to
bitesize the profound
or they'll keep
scrolling down.

MASTERS OF THE CLOAK

What brilliant architects of routine we are,
consummate constructors of regularity.

Oh, how we've become so masterful at
cloaking the strangeness of our existence.

HISTORY OF THE SAOL

THE FOURTH EPIPHANY

The fourth of such epiphanies is that we can experience moments of beauty *and* moments of suffering simultaneously—and this is also the case for moments of ugliness and moments of suffering. This is intuitive and is encapsulated by the widespread claim that people have experienced *great beauty in suffering.*

Yet, there is a difference in the way that judgments of the beautiful and judgments of the ugly individually interact with suffering. Namely, our judgments of the beautiful *alleviate*, while our judgments of the ugly *exacerbate.*

Once again, keep in mind that our aesthetic judgments are elicited only by the very phenomenon of beauty or ugliness within the world—we cannot elicit the judgments of our own free will.

Experiences of beauty serve to *alleviate* one's suffering by eliciting that instinctual, immediate, and pre-rational *acceptance* of our condition as suffering beings. It is not a physical alleviation, but rather, one of existential alleviation—as it is the case that an unjustified suffering is worse than a justified one. It would add further fuel to our mental torment, *to know that the suffering we had felt had served no purpose.* But, with a suffering justified by both the existence of beauty and also the possibility of having aesthetic judgments of that beauty, the power of our suffering is weakened—"I am a suffering being, but I am also a beauty-perceiving being. If I have to suffer in exchange for these moments of being beholden to the beauty of music and art and dance and nature, then let me suffer! If experiences of beauty must manifest within a suffering being, then let me suffer!"

Experiences of the ugly serve to *exacerbate* one's suffering by eliciting that instinctual, immediate, and pre-rational *rejection* of our condition as suffering beings. Once again, this exacerbation is of the existential kind—for, unjustified suffering is worse than a justified one. When we perceive what's ugly—that within the world which, when judged aesthetically tilts us toward the *'No!'* to the question *'Is Being better than Nothing?'*—we are now left as *beings that merely suffer*—as opposed to *beings that both suffer and experience beauty* (as is the case in our aesthetic judgments of beauty). The former (*a merely suffering being*) is a bleak existence. "I am a suffering being, and yet, if all that surrounds me is ugly—death, disease, and the existence of evil—then truly, what is the point in my persisting?"

It follows that experiences of the beautiful and experiences of the ugly *cannot* be simultaneously experienced together. They are completely separate phenomena. Experiences of the beautiful result in a justification for our condition as suffering beings, while experiences of the ugly result in a dissolution of prior accumulated justification—or alternatively, provides justification for death. Our being beholden to either phenomenon results in opposite answers to the moral question of ontology, and the *'Yes!'* and the *'No!'* cannot be simultaneously proclaimed.

INEFFABLE

Synchronicity:

When externalities are aligned
to such a degree that it seems as
though it had been touched by
the intervening hands of the divine.

SHAKE ON IT

Reality promises to give
you what you want if you
ask for it with action.

WORDS UPON A PAGE

What is it to write?

When consciousness fertilizes the
unconscious womb of the brain,
birthing linguistic patterns
the world has never seen.

BLOODIED INK

When the quill runs dry,
only one solution remains:

Jam the quill into my chest
and watch my heart spray
the white of the paper
completely red.

PAINTER

Passion and purpose
are the pillars of
human attraction.

THROUGH THE LENS

Our world is already an
impressive landscape of art;
the photographer merely isolates it.

HISTORY OF THE SAOL

THE FIFTH, SIXTH, &
SEVENTH EPIPHANY

HISTORY OF THE SAOL: THE FIFTH, SIXTH, & SEVENTH EPIPHANY

The fifth of such epiphanies is that suffering has retrospective purpose, which is *to have beckoned, and ultimately revealed the hidden Being of beauty*—a phenomenon that must have emerged from out of the unconscious, collective human attempt to construct a phenomenon that would both alleviate and justify inextricable suffering—in short, *to produce a solution to the problem of suffering.*

For ask yourself two questions:

How could the collective human spirit live alongside an inextricable suffering without any justification? This would not at all be possible. There would be widespread renunciation without any form of metaphysical justification for our condition as suffering beings.

And further, how could beauty have emerged without the problem of suffering? We had to discover beauty by unconsciously birthing it, namely, by developing our capacity to perceive it with aesthetic judgments. Is it not a curious fact that aesthetic judgments of beauty are a wholly human affair? Yes of course, animals feel suffering, but animals are also conditioned with innate justification, justification that is inherently built in, which takes the form of an overwhelming life drive that cannot be rejected. Aesthetic judgments made by animals are merely responses to stimulus, instinct, and preservation, as opposed to the contemplative enterprise that makes up human aesthetic judgments. This is similarly the case for the difference in the relation animals and humans have with their suffering—for humans this relation is contemplative, for animals it is not. Humans are beings that are *aware* of the moral question of ontology, and this separates us from other suffering beings, insofar as we need more than mere innate justification (life drive) as metaphysical grounding for our proclamations of the *'Yes!'* or the *'No!'* Humans are capable of rejecting this innate life drive (this is found in our capacity for suicide). So, the question above becomes: *How then, did beauty emerge as a result of the problem of suffering?*

This is how the phenomenon of beauty was unconsciously birthed. First, it is the case that single-celled organisms do *not* have the capacity to make aesthetic judgments of beauty, while all humans do. Thus, somewhere along the trajectory of evolutionary history, from single-celled organisms to humans, the phenomenon of beauty must have emerged (somewhere closer in time to the appearance of *Homo sapiens),* and further, was so incredibly adaptive that it became a universalized characteristic of the human species itself. The phenomenon of beauty is a recipe that first re-quires earlier and less sophisticated cognitive tools of aesthetic judgment—attraction perceptions of symmetry and asymmetry in sexual selection, colour perception for gathering ripe and edible fruits and vegetables, and recognition of plush, hospitable land versus hostile, arid land (the oasis among an African desert). These primitive aesthetic judgments were adaptive for obvious reasons but did not extend to the *whole* of the external world—they were not generalizable or structured into a holistic phenom-enon of beauty, rather they were discrete cognitive tools with specific purpose. As the evolutionary timeline neared *Homo sapi-ens,* the cognitive power of our ancient ancestors increased. With this increase in cognitive power, proto-humans became more cog-nizant of the inextricable feature of suffering—producing an offshoot problem, namely, the problem of cognized suffering, the problem of how to justify human existence given its intrinsic re-lationship to, and awareness of suffering. The brain thus adapted, amalgamating the previously developed cognitive tools for *spe-cific* aesthetic judgment into the *holistic* phenomenon of beauty (with the use of those tools stated above, and surely, other cognitive tools of aesthetic judgment left unstated). In the past, these tools had been associated with the alleviation of suffering, or at least the experience of pleasure—mating with a partner, staving off hunger pains, establishing a settlement at an oasis in a desert, and so on. So, why wouldn't the brain then turn to these cognitive tools for an answer to this new emergent problem of suffering? The biological predisposition for this new emergent phenomenon was normally distributed (bell curved) across the human species—meaning some were hyper-aesthetic judgers of beauty, some were hypo-aesthetic judgers of beauty, and most were in the middle. Eventually, the phenomenon became widespread and ultimately universalized, as a result of its incredibly adaptive quality within an environment so inextricably tied up with suffering. Those that were able to judge beauty could justify their existence and continue to find meaning in their everyday survival. Those that were unable to judge beauty developed proto-depression and proto-nihilism—which are unquestionably non-adaptive states of mind. The phenomenon of beauty, or more accurately, our aesthetic judgment of the external world as being beautiful, serves the survival function of quelling our increased cognizance of inevitable and inextricable suffering. As a result, proto-humans continued their participation in the game of life—reproduction, survival, and technological and cultural advancement—but now with an additional element of meaning.

And thus, the sixth of such epiphanies is that suffering must have necessarily come before beauty in the trajectory of both emerging phenomena and human existence. This is because beauty—being a wholly human affair—had to have been created by our collective spirit as a tool for question-posing consciousness to contend with suffering! This is not contentious—suffering has been around for much longer than consciousness capable of making aesthetic judgments of beauty.

And finally, the seventh of such epiphanies is that the development of our capacity for being beholden to beauty was a collective and unconscious bursting forth of the phenomenon of beauty from out of our struggle to *overcome immemorial suffering*. Thereby, making our aesthetic judgments of beauty the instinctual, immediate, and pre-rational answer to the problem of suffering—the metaphysical grounding for our justification of the *'Yes!'* to the question *'Is Being better than Nothing?'* It is the evolutionary solution to the problem of becoming *aware* of the inevitability and inextricability of suffering, a problem that has yet to manifest for non-human animals.

FAUX GOD

We lie because we
are arrogant enough
to assume that we
can control reality.

But, reality has a nice
way of revealing to us
that we are utterly
impotent in the face
of existence.

ICARUS

Yes, it is true that light
is produced by the sun.

But make no mistake,
it is human consciousness
that lights up existence.

FORGED

You ask,
"How is a hero forged?"

The hero is distinguished
from the rest by means
of one consistent action:

The hero always answers the question—
How will you respond to this fear?
with a definitive,

"I will face it!"

MAN'S BEST FRIEND

Politics is as important
to us as barking and
sniffing asses is to a dog:

Inescapable human behaviour.

EARTHLY ORCHESTRA

Yes,
and in the end,
I'll sing as loud
as thunder tones
the sounds and notes
of impassioned storms
to raise up souls,
harmoniously beside
roaring horns
and trumpet cries
that bellows life
into our soulless world.

REBIRTH

It is through passion and passion only
that we come to life for the second time.

This discovery is our
birth after birth—
our second cry
when we realize
that life can be
affirmed!

HISTORY OF THE SAOL

THE EIGHTH EPIPHANY

Both an alienation from the beautiful and a devotion to the ugly can result from great suffering.

When one greatly suffers either mentally, physically, spiritually, or otherwise, they can become alienated from the beautiful—consciously or unconsciously. This is the case because for the overwhelming sufferer, it is almost impossible for them to see beauty within the world *in light of their suffering*. Why? Because the overwhelming sufferer *does not want to justify* their terrible suffering, and to see beauty *is* to justify it. Instead, an attempt (conscious or unconscious) will be made to alienate themselves from that which justifies the thing they want least justified. And furthermore, to alienate themselves from the *project of justification* itself.

This is the root of our alienation from the beautiful—the root of our attempt to blind ourselves to the beauty in the world.

When one greatly suffers either mentally, physically, spiritually, or otherwise, they can become devoted to the ugly. This will happen when the overwhelming sufferer experiences such great pain that they begin to condemn the world that has been shown to be sufficiently conditioned for the existence of the great pain that they must endure. To condemn the world is of course to say that, it is, in fact, *Nothing* that is better than *Being*—or similarly to proclaim a reverberating *'No!'* to the moral question of ontology. In this, the corrupted aim to *justify* nothingness develops. This is to devote oneself to the ugly, to see only what's ugly in the world, dissolving any remaining justification they once had for life—a step in the direction of suicide or destruction.

CANDLE

We are fleshy bipedal creatures
that house the capacity to
beautifully create.

But, only for a relative sliver of
time, and then we succumb to the
cold embrace of nothingness.

We are flickering tools of
innovation for the universe.

Every day is Halloween
except Halloween itself.

For, tonight we remove our
ordered masks and our true
absurdist nature comes out!

SCARCE

Good conversation is in high demand,
yet, greatly low in supply.

Keep those that provide
such conversational sustenance
close at hand.

Their value is immense and irreplaceable.

Wake up, coffee, work,
commute, dinner, Netflix,
sex, sleep, repeat. All this
hangs on by mere thread,
and only a tug of reflection
is sufficient enough to reveal
that our waking life is as
absurd as our dreams.

THE I

The strange thing about humans
is that each of us evade definition
while we live, breathe, and beat—
only at the time of our death is our
book closed, solidifying the *I* into
an unalterable object.

HISTORY OF THE SAOL

THE FINAL EPIPHANY

HISTORY OF THE SAOL: THE FINAL EPIPHANY

The final of such epiphanies is that the trajectory of the human
spirit is moving toward a complete alienation from the beautiful
as a result of the corruption of its aims, its *ends*. We are *neglecting*
the beauty solution—the solution that our species had produced
from out of the millennia of human interaction with an external
world. Furthermore, we are slowly becoming feverish devotees of
the ugly—willingly enveloping ourselves in metaphysical justifi-
cation of the *'No!'*

This is an unquestionably devastating destination given the
primary function of the beautiful and the nihilistic function of the
ugly.

The trajectory of collective human consciousness has become
undirected—the unrestrained consumption of superficial and bar-
ren entertainment, the unrestrained pursuit of material wealth, the
unrestrained pursuit of industrial expansion, and so on. All of
these pursuits are without any regard for the devastating effects
that result from our gluttonous media consumption, our insatiable
greed, and the further reduction of humanity into algorithmic
functions.

These pursuits are corrupted insofar as they are devoid of the
fundamental and guiding moral principle that had conditioned the
human spirit from time immemorial: *to justify our condition as
suffering beings.* Instead, our guiding principles have become *me-
dia distraction, greed, narcissism,* and *ideological possession*—
the guiding principles upon which our modern society is built.
This is not to say that we don't *believe* our aims are conditioned
by the fundamental principle; rather, it is merely to say that we
are looking in the *wrong place.*

Without anywhere to turn to justify our condition as suffering beings, we are beginning to believe that our suffering is *too heavy a burden to bear.* Consequently, we are caught in the thrall of this alienation process—the process whereby we *choose* to blind ourselves to beauty in a revolt against the project of justification itself. It is the vicious spiral of modernity: We look for justification in the wrong places in an attempt to alleviate our modern industrial suffering, then our suffering becomes too great a burden to bear insofar as it is left unjustified, and finally, in a profound defiance of an existence so insufferable, we turn our backs on the project of justification altogether—ultimately turning our backs on the beauty solution as well (either consciously or unconsciously). This process is quickly spiraling out of control. The human spirit is beginning to lose faith in the project of justification and in time, will come to believe that suffering, in being so unbearable, *ought not* be justified at all.

It is no wonder that rates of depression, anxiety, and suicide are rampant—that we live in a world where someone takes their own life every forty seconds, that over two thousand people, every day, feel that the weight of life is too great to bear and choose suicide as their answer. Ask yourself: *What does eight hundred thousand suicides per year stand for when just one is too many?*

Not only have we stripped our society bare of justification for the *'Yes!'* as a result of our corrupted pursuits—we have turned our backs on its most potent form: *beauty.* And in doing so, the *'No!'* is taking firm hold over the collective spirit of humanity.

MEANINGLESS PLACES

The tyranny of meaningless environments
reveals the existential dictum that one must
strive to create a way of life that justifies the
suffering of the human condition.

It is a paradoxical situation because
the meaningless environment is the
least capable of justifying this unavoidable
suffering that we all face.

Nonetheless, knowing the dictum—
*that the way you choose to live your life will
either justify or exacerbate suffering*—
is enough to drive you toward your passion,
pursue your dreams, and transcend your pain.

ABRAHAM AND ISAAC

Sometimes your future self calls upon
the present you to kill what is loved most—
that without a sacrifice of this magnitude,
that by clinging to your love of the present you,
you inadvertently murder your highest potential.

SORROW OR SOLUTION

Is there so great
a suffering that even
beauty cannot
be perceived?

A SKELETON'S POTENTIAL

I am a bag of bones that has done the impossible—
I have injected divinity into a dying star
becoming a creative mouthpiece
for the infinite.

I am resurrected.

HISTORY OF
THE SAOL

A WAY OF LIFE

HISTORY OF THE SAOL: A WAY OF LIFE

"With these epiphanies in mind the Master tasked himself with constructing a *way of life* aligned with the epiphanies that he had experienced. The first of which was to discard the Buddhist idea that the alleviation of suffering consists in the dissolution of all attachment—for this is renunciation in disguise. Instead, he had a new idea—a new *set of aims*—that people had to *become art!* And, one morning he burst through the kitchen door, and cried aloud, *'A world starved of beauty cries out for each of us to become art!'*

"A mantra if there ever was one! The aim was to *engage* in life! Not to resign from it. The moral act consisted in creating and disseminating the very phenomenon that the human spirit had struggled for millennia to establish as a universal cure—as our oasis—as our refuge! In creating beauty, one overcomes their own suffering; in disseminating beauty, one tilts the world toward the *'Yes!'*

"To the Master, it had become patently obvious what the religions of the world had unknowingly professed—they first declared the *suffering axiom,* and then their answer was to write beautiful scripture, verse, and prose—to create beautiful myths, stories, and parables. To create beautiful masterworks of art—art that was overbearing in its *'Yes!'* to life! To build the greatest architecture the world had ever laid eyes upon. In short, to live *poetically, artistically,* and thus, *beautifully!* That is what the Master so distinctly felt as he surrounded himself with those imposing cathedrals, mosques, synagogues, and temples. Those brief sparks of life he felt were the immediate and instinctual *'Yeses!'* bellowing loudly from within the deep soul of the human species! The religions pursued... created... disseminated... and thus, they *overcame!*

"He had finally found the thread that weaved its way through those nine splendid epiphanies. That in overcoming one's suffering by dedicating oneself to creating beauty, and further, in disseminating this beauty across the world—so that the whole of humanity could awaken with the rising sun, *wholly justified in their waking*—he had discovered, all along, what our artistic ancestors had encapsulated so magnificently in their masterpieces: proof that the human species *itself* could become beautiful! And further, that *we must!*

"This transformed into the Master's fundamental aim: *to become beautiful by transforming his consciousness into a conduit for the tilt toward the positive answer!* To sacrifice himself to the positive answer to the question written above *Joy of Life*—the question etched deep within our hearts! To become a *'Yes!'* to the question: *'Is Being better than Nothing?'*

"And, that is what he did, with the help of his servant. He exhausted all of his resources, many decades ago, to buy this abandoned university campus and littered it with artwork that professed the *'Yes!'* To have artists reside at the compound, under his patronage, to create masterworks of the *'Yes!'* This was the first step: *to create something beautiful*—he had transformed a dilapidated university campus into a refuge of beauty.

"The Master came to this university with his servant—who by now you might have guessed had been Amhrán all along—and established the compound. After establishing the compound, he no longer had work here to do. The earliest Saol had already become firm in their belief of his nine epiphanies—and could thus continue the legacy. He felt his work at the compound was complete and that his time had come to venture out into the dark, embittered corners, beyond the forest, forever out into the world of the *'No!'* to dedicate his life, revealing the hidden cure of beauty in an effort to tilt the world back to life. For it is not enough for one to merely revel in beauty, one must also encourage others to do so as well! In doing so, he had achieved the second step: *to disseminate beauty.* In creating and disseminating, he had finally accomplished his fundamental aim—the goal that had been entailed within the nine epiphanies: *to become beautiful himself—to turn his consciousness into a masterwork of art*—so that as he suffered he could look *within* for alleviation. The Master's final words to his servant were sparse but profound. *'Your life matters, even in the grand scheme of things, for your life is one of many answers to the question: 'Is Being better than Nothing?' And in the end, when all answers come forth, spanning all corners of Earth, let's hope the human spirit screams aloud a reverberating 'Yes!'*

"Amhrán the servant is an older man now, and in some years, will himself be upon the threshold of death. He is the last remaining among us who had interacted with the Master and when Amhrán perishes, the Master will become but a myth.

"It was many years ago now, that the Master had sojourned into the world of the *'No!'* Since then, the Saol people have been fulfilling the Master's moral prescription—that when we mature in age, we must first *create* something beautiful, beginning our life-long devotion to the *'Yes!'* and then we must follow in the footsteps of the Master, venturing into the world of the *'No!'* to embark on the Saol *pilgrimage of dissemination*—the wholly personal pilgrimage to find the *sick*—and to cure their incessant *'No!'* with beauty. In doing so, we *become* beautiful and transcend the suffering of humanity, by justifying our lives, and becoming accepting of our condition as suffering beings!"

The lecture had finally come to a close. My gracious guide had finished the history with fire ablaze in both eyes, with deep reds that coloured the skin of his beaming face—*two flame-filled eyes that spoke a fullness of life, two blood-coloured cheeks that spoke a redness of heart.*

THE MASTER'S FIRST PROCLAMATION:

A SAOL VERSE

A world starved of beauty cries
out for each of us to become art!

THE MASTER'S SECOND PROCLAMATION:

A SAOL VERSE

Your life matters,
even in the grand scheme of things,
for your life is one of many answers
to the question:
'Is Being better than Nothing?'

And in the end,
when all answers come forth,
spanning all corners of Earth,
let's hope the human spirit
screams aloud a reverberating
'Yes!'

THE SAOL PRAYER OF PURPOSE

Beauty:

Create it,
disseminate it,
become it.

THE SAOL PRAYER OF GRATITUDE

Let us thank reality for
providing us with the
antidote to suffering:
Beauty.

HISTORY OF THE SAOL

MY DEPARTURE FROM THE SAOL COMPOUND

MY DEPARTURE FROM THE SAOL COMPOUND

When I left the compound after seven days and seven nights, I hadn't felt any different—that is, on the surface.

Though, I noticed that during my return trip, I picked up the pen with newfound fervor.

I'll never forget the only thing that Amhrán said to me while I stayed with his people.

It was during the seventh night as I was packing my belongings for my return home. To my surprise, Amhrán—a man in his early sixties, with salt and peppered hair and a distinctly jovial expression—slowly walked into my lodgings, picked up my little notepad of quotes, placed the pad into the cold palm of my hand, and with a warm smile had whispered but one word.

"Write."

Though, at the time, I did not understand what he meant by this simple instruction, I now know that he knew I had been conditioned, that the seed—a guiding principle—had been planted. That now, the 'Yes!' would only take a matter of time.

As I was leaving the compound, I turned around and took one final glance at the Picasso-like sculpture I had encountered earlier that week. I was surprised to see that the sculpture had taken on a new form. Although the disfigured face still resembled a man of great suffering, his two marble lips were now curled into a small and subtle smile—a small and subtle smile just like the one the Master had worn after he had made the choice to stay alive— as if all the suffering in the world could stand no chance against a life so profoundly justified, against a life so utterly accepted. And it was in this moment that my cheeks filled with a great buzz of unfamiliar sensation, overwhelmed with ecstatic waves of hitherto unknown joy. Yes, it was in this moment that my two lips moved in a momentous muscular motion upward to form my very own small and subtle smile.

A SMALL SEED

What follows is what I wrote while seated aboard the airplane, coming home from that strange and distant land overseas.

I want to scream out that the world is beautiful, but who would hear me with ears to their own whispering mouths?

I want to scream out that the world is beautiful, but I fear that the word *ugly* will find its way out.

I want to scream out that the world is beautiful, but what if I only manage to mouth four soundless words with a stream of helpless tears?

I want to scream out that the world is beautiful, but will I be slashed to pieces at the hands of those who refuse to accept, with their sharpened blades of resentment?

I want to scream out that the world is beautiful, but is this just a lie that I sing into my own pleading mind?

I want to scream out that the world is beautiful, but maybe if I do the whole world will flash before my eyes, in a profound display of its tortured spirit.

Maybe the world is broken.

Maybe I am the kid who mends his broken toy with tape and glue and pretends it's as good as new, but in reality, I am playing with undifferentiated pieces on the cold, wooden floor.

I want to scream out that the world is beautiful, even if my scream is a delusional mess.

I want to scream out that the world is beautiful, in its misery, in its suffering, if it's hell.

I want to scream out that the world is beautiful because that is what makes it so—yes, *our scream, our plea, our crying on our knees!*

Yes!

I'll scream.

Will you?

"Write."

THE END

A visceral war wages on in our hearts between Being and Nothingness. The very struggle of the human is this ontological conflict—the human is constantly at the threshold of this inner struggle—a struggle that determines the guiding principle that will become the foundation for all individual action. So, it is thus, imperative to peer inward and ask yourself the question: *Which force prevails?*

What are the two outcomes?

Either we create, disseminate, and ultimately become beauty. And, in doing so, we justify Being, with all its suffering. Otherwise, Nothingness becomes the seductive option—*"Let us become a profound and rebellious annihilation of Being—this is the only way to avoid unavoidable suffering!"* This is the logic of the nihilist—the Advocate of Nothingness.

At all costs, we must regard this second option as anti-human—for the consequence of following through with this logic is the annihilation of consciousness and all that is wondrously entailed—beauty, love, truth, friendship, conversation, music, art, poetry, purpose, and the experience of consciousness itself.

To which end does the world tilt?

For now, toward *Being*.

But, the twentieth century has shown that Nothingness has a great hold over the spirit of humanity. Perhaps this is the consequence of our condition as beings moving toward death—of our condition as beings moving toward Nothingness. We are beings

that succumb—that at every moment the great culminating disso-
lution of the self looms heavily overhead. But, we must
remember, *we are not nothing, we are something!*

Humans have two fundamental powers: creation and destruc-
tion. The Advocate of Being and the Advocate of Nothingness are
conditioned by both. The question becomes: *How do the powers
manifest within each?*

First: *creation.*

For the Advocate of Being, creation is the main power of op-
eration—creating masterworks of art, writing, music and
architecture; creating innovative tools and technological advance-
ments that make our lives easier (beginning with stone tools,
moving toward computers, and modern medicine), and addition-
ally, to take us further into the far reaches of our curiosity. The
aim is to justify, alleviate, and ultimately, dissolve suffering!

For the Advocate of Nothingness, the creative capacity is cor-
rupted. They create suffering to further justify their logic against
Being. And there is no shortage of human created suffering—a
glimpse at the horrors of Nazi Germany is evidence enough. The
Advocate of Nothingness wants nothing more than imminent ex-
tinction.

Next: *destruction.*

For the Advocate of Nothingness, destruction is their main
source of power. How terrible, that one of the fundamental powers
of humanity is the capacity to dissolve the consciousness of the
other, and also, of the self. The Advocate of Nothingness uses
their logic to justify why they ought to destroy consciousness—
this manifests as suicide, or potentially murder and genocide.

Conversely, the Advocate of Being utilizes a weaker form of destruction. They attempt to convince Advocates of Nothingness that the *Nothing logic* is flawed in an attempt to convert—and thus, if successful, destroying *forms* of corrupted consciousness rather than destroying the entire being itself.

No one person is a pure advocate of either force. We all partake in this constant struggle, being tugged toward both Being and Nothingness. None of us escape death, and our distinct awareness of this will serve to perpetuate the tug of the Nothing. We succumb and we are aware that we succumb. This is our predicament.

I look out the window and see a dove dancing in the grass. This dancing dove is a pure Advocate of Being—it does not question its existence and so it cannot reject it. The dove effortlessly dances the dance of Being, without a misstep. See, doves are built to dance, but, *humans are different.* It is hard for humans to dance the dance of Being, for the human is in a constant questioning of the dance itself, and this questioning, if taken too far, will inevitably tilt the whole of humanity toward negation.

But, we need to destroy, for how else will we destroy death itself? And, ask yourself, *is this not our destiny?*

To destroy death itself, the being in question must be the type of being that is perpetually aware of the shadow of its own demise. And, as far as we know, we are the only ones capable of such awareness. This is what the human species moves toward—*this is our dance—the dance of Dasein!* From out of this dance emerges the spirit of our Being! To attain a beautiful immortality without suffering! To collectively join hands in a triumphant rejection of the Nothing!

First, we populate the stars with illusory Gods—then we strive to become them! We *are* beings moving toward death, but more so, we are beings *becoming* the Gods! This is the telos of the human spirit—so long as our ethos remains that of Being over Nothingness.

To this end, let this book stand as my advocacy of Being, my affirmation of life, and my hope that the dance of Dasein rages on.

THE END

AFTERWORD

DASEIN, SUICIDE, & BEAUTY

AFTERWORD: DASEIN, SUICIDE, & BEAUTY

DASEIN

Dasein is a philosophical term that was popularized in the ground-breaking *Being and Time* [*Sein und Zeit*], an existential magnum opus written in 1927 by the prominent twentieth-century German philosopher Martin Heidegger. Dasein is a German word that directly translates to *being-there*. But Heidegger adamantly warns against our understanding of Dasein through this translation, specifically in its use as a mere substitute for consciousness (Dreyfus, 1990, p. 13). As Heidegger said,

"Any attempt [...] to rethink Being and Time is thwarted as long as one is satisfied with the observation that, in this study, the term 'being there' is used in place of 'consciousness.' As if it were simply a matter of using different words! [...] 'Being there' names that which should first of all be experienced, and subsequently thought of, as a place, namely, the location of the truth of Being." (Heidegger, 1943, p. 213)[1]

To understand Dasein then, we must look toward something more basic than *'mental states and intentionality'* (Dreyfus, 1990, p. 14). Dreyfus recommends that Dasein should be understood as the distinctive *Being* that is particular to the human being (Dreyfus, 1990, p. 14). But, this raises the question: *What is it that characterizes the Being that is particular to the human being?* There are two inextricable features of Dasein.

[1]   The First Feature: The Question of its own Being

First, Heidegger intuitively recognizes that out of the totality of different beings that exist—atoms, photons, and quarks; tables, chairs, and houses; asteroids, planets, and stars—it is *only* for the

---

[1] Heidegger, *The Way Back into the Ground of Metaphysics,* as cited in *Existentialism from Dostoyevsky to Sartre* by Walter Kaufmann, 1960.

human being that the *question of its own Being* arises, becoming its issue.

"Dasein [...] is ontically distinguished by the fact that, in its very Being, that Being is an issue for it" (Heidegger, 1927, p. 32).

This simply means that it is humans alone that are concerned with what it means to *be,* with what it means to *exist*—that sticks and stones and all other objects are utterly indifferent to their being a stick or a stone or an object (Mulhall, 1996, p. 15). Why, then, is Dasein concerned with its own Being?

To understand the concern that Dasein has toward its own Being, it is imperative to make the distinction between the *essence* of Dasein and the *essence* of other such non-Dasein beings (i.e., motorcycles, water molecules, iPhones, and so on). This draws upon one of the most fundamental claims in the school of existential thought, that for Dasein—the human being—*existence precedes essence.* And for non-Dasein objects, this equation is reversed such that *their essence precedes their existence.* What does this mean? A simple way to conceptualize this distinction is to compare an object with a human. Right now, I am holding a pen in my hand. Within my mind, I can begin to construct the necessary and sufficient conditions of what it means to be *a pen.* It is an instrument that writes with ink, it is typically cylindrical, it has a ballpoint, and so on. Eventually, I will hit upon the *essence of pen-ness,* namely, in having laid out its constituent features. Now, let us imagine that all pens suddenly vanished from Earth. In this case, the existing entities that we call *pen* no longer exist—yet, the essence of pen-ness remains within our minds, as a mental model built from its constituent features. If I were then to construct a pen, I could build it from this mental model (the essence of the pen). In such a case, its essence not only preceded the existence of the new pen but further guided the production of the pen itself, aiding in its coming into existence.

This, however, is not the case for Dasein. As I have previously indicated, for Dasein *existence precedes essence.* This means that the *what-ness*—the necessary and sufficient features of a thing—

cannot be laid out for a human being (Mulhall, 1996, p. 15). Dasein evades a preceding what-ness altogether, insofar as Dasein is born *before* it is defined. Consequently, Dasein is not a *what* but a *who*—whose essence is shaped only through the choices it makes *while existing through time* (Critchley, *On Mineness,* 2009). Dasein partakes in the project of *what itself is* and *what itself will become*—a project that is alien to ordinary objects (Mulhall, 1996, p. 15). A pen is a pen and does not partake in its becoming a pen.

In short, Dasein's essence is contained within its possibilities and choices, that, at every moment, Dasein has a *multiplicity of possibilities*—an array of possible ways of being—and in choosing from this multiplicity, Dasein *becomes* (Mulhall, 1996, p. 15).

Thus, Dasein's *project of essence defining* serves as an answer to our previous question: *Why is Dasein concerned with its own Being?* Unlike other beings who have a definitive essence, Dasein must strive to create one in its very existing. Because of this fact, Dasein's concern *must* be tied up with its possibilities and choices, insofar as that is where its essence will be derived. Dasein must decide for itself *what it ought to become* (should I *be* this or that?)—not only a question it must ask itself, but a question that cannot omit the *issue of Being* (Mulhall, 1996, p. 15).

However, there is a second reason that conditions Dasein's concern for the question of its own Being. It is because death hangs over Dasein—like the Sword of Damocles—as the always possible impossibility of Dasein, which thus ends Dasein's project of essence defining, that Dasein also has to wonder *when it will cease to be* (I could die at any moment—right now, tomorrow, or in ten years!) "As soon as man comes to life, he is at once old enough to die" (Heidegger, 1927, p. 289).

This *ought* for what Dasein will become and this *wondering* for when Dasein will cease to be are both inextricably tied up with Dasein's concern for its own Being.

[2]   The Second Feature: Mineness

Second, Heidegger stresses the concept of *mineness* [*Jemeinig-keit*]. This feature of Dasein refers to the fact that the Being of Dasein is always experienced as an experience that is *mine* (Critchley, *On Mineness,* 2009). This means that each individual's experience of being human occurs through the lens of the first person. And, these questions of *What ought I to become?* and *When will I cease to be?* are always *only* an issue for *me*. The former question is resolved only through *my* existence, and the latter question is *my ownmost* possibility—in other words, only *I* can die my own death, no one can choose to die for me.

————⌒————

THE WORLD

Being-in-the-world

According to Heidegger, our conceptualization of Dasein must re-frain from decontextualizing Dasein from its world. This is to say that we must not isolate Dasein from the place in which it lives. The Being of Dasein is also the world, such that "the world is part and parcel of [its] Being, of the fabric of [its] existence" (Critch-ley, *On Being-in-the-world,* 2009). This is because, as we have seen, Dasein's essence manifests from out of the choices that Dasein makes—and to make choices is to necessarily *be contained within a world where choices can be made.* Without a *place,* whereby Dasein can exercise its capacity to choose and thus actualize its possibilities, the essence of Dasein could never be realized. This is the grounds for Heidegger's idea of *being-in-the-world* [*In-der-Welt-sein*]—Dasein is thrown [*geworfen*] into a context, history, and world of contingencies whereby it must man-ifest its essence through existing. Insofar as the essence of Dasein is contingent upon the world into which it has been thrown, it makes sense why Heidegger adamantly expressed concerns against decontextualizing Dasein. Dasein and the world are inextricably linked—this is a fact. And yet, the contingent context, history, and time of the world serve to set the parameters for Dasein's possibilities—we never get to choose when we are born, yet, we immediately adopt the rules of the prevailing culture, strive after conceptions of success defined by our culture, adopt the contemporary dialect, and so on.

It is important to note that the *mood* [*Stimmung*] Dasein has toward the world is not one of indifference. As a consequence of Dasein's engagement with the world, in its effort to work out its essence through time, Dasein's mood must be one of *care* [*Sorge*]. More precisely, we cannot help but create and execute plans and projects that both make use of the objects in the world and act in an awareness, consideration, and involvement with other people (Critchley, *On Being-in-the-world,* 2009).

------⟨∞⟩------

DEATH

Being-towards-death, Authenticity, and Anxiety

The crux of Dasein, however, is found within its relation to death. Death, as previously stated, is the always possible impossibility of Dasein—or put more simply, the fact that at any given moment *I* could cease to be, that this cessation of the *I* that is wholly mine is an inevitability, and that only *I* can die my own death (Critchley, *On Death,* 2009). This represents Heidegger's concept of *being-towards-death* [*Sein-zum-Tode*].

There are two modes of being that Dasein can take towards death: *authenticity* or *inauthenticity* (Critchley, *On Mineness,* 2009). Heidegger tells us that *authenticity* [*Eigentlichkeit*] is a mode of being achieved through Dasein's experience of *anxiety* [*Angst*]. Though, this is not the type of anxiety that is spoken of in our modern psychological project. Dasein's anxiety is one that is directed at the inevitable possibility of a world devoid of Dasein's existence—a world without *me*. However, a defining characteristic of Dasein's anxiety is that it is not an anxiety of anything in particular—namely, it is not directed toward a definitive being (Critchley, *On Anxiety,* 2009). Instead, its object is that of nothingness, annihilation, or the cessation of possibility—it is an anxiety of *being-in-the-world* as such (Critchley, *On Anxiety,* 2009). These are not *things* in the proper sense—the object of anxiety is indefinite and found in *"nothing and nowhere"* (Critchley, *On Anxiety,* 2009). This undifferentiated anxiety produces an overwhelming feeling of *no longer being at home in the world*—what Heidegger calls an *uncanny [unheimlich]* feeling, insofar as the "everyday world slips away" and "our home becomes strange" (Critchley, *On Anxiety,* 2009).

Anxiety is a *fundamental mood [Grundstimmung]* for Dasein because it is through this anxiety that the kind of being that Dasein *is* becomes disclosed—that our most essential possibility is death (I *may* become a psychologist or a writer, but I will most certainly die). It is through this anxiety that Dasein reveals to itself that it is an *individuating being*—as something different than other things—not a thing with a definitive essence, but rather, and in stark contrast with everything else, a finite being that is *becoming*—a *who* not a *what* (Critchley, *On Anxiety,* 2009). This awareness of the distinct difference between Dasein and all other things is made manifest in our feeling apart from everything else, in our feeling apart from the world.

Counterintuitively, this unsettling feeling we have toward death—usually considered unwanted—ought to be welcomed as a potentially transformative mood that can bring us into connection with what we truly are—*a finite and free who* (Critchley, *On Anxiety,* 2009). Heidegger believes that only through this understanding of what we are, may we achieve *existential self-possession*—namely, our taking ownership of our actions, thoughts and possibilities. This is the necessary step into authenticity.

Conversely, *inauthentic* [*uneigentlich*] Dasein exhibits *fear* of death and strives toward distractions in *the They* [*das Man*] that both prevent Dasein from having to become existentially self-possessed.

Heidegger tells us that fear is distinct from anxiety because fear is a fear of something in particular—of some threatening being in the world (i.e., violent storms, wild predators, and so on) (Critchley, *On Anxiety,* 2009). However, in having fear toward death, Dasein turns its own death into an *event to occur in the distant future,* as opposed to what it really is, which is the always present possibility of Dasein's impossibility. In *fear* of death, the Being of Dasein is not disclosed as a *being-towards-death,* and as a result Dasein turns its back on its own finitude, *tranquilizing* itself from having to relate to its death. Consequently, Dasein fails to open itself up to the multiplicity of possibilities, thus failing to achieve existential self-possession, freedom, and authenticity.

But this is the nature of the inauthentic, to avoid ownership of one's actions, thoughts, and possibilities—to reject the existential responsibility that Dasein would otherwise have to uphold with an awareness of its freedom to choose—freedom that entails the unsettling feelings of anxiety and homelessness. Instead, inauthentic Dasein desires and strives to retain the comfort of existential ignorance and naiveté.

SUICIDE

Heidegger remains quiet on the topic of suicide. This is puzzling because it seems that suicide is yet another Dasein-only possibility—so much so that Heidegger's omission could have been none other than intentional. Nonetheless, it is clear that only Dasein can make the choice to self-annihilate, a decision that derives from the belief that being a being is *worse* than being nothing at all. The question then becomes whether the choice to self-annihilate is of an authentic or inauthentic mode of being.

The intuitive answer is that suicide is inauthentic. But, the analysis must go deeper than what our first impressions indicate.

For one, to be suicidal-Dasein about to self-annihilate is to also be in a full awareness of one's finitude. This is because the project of self-annihilation is one that necessarily entails an understanding of one's finitude. For implicit in the act of *self-annihilation* is the very possibility of being able to be destroyed. Namely, suicide would not be an option for Dasein if Dasein could not die. Counterintuitively, this would point to suicide as being authentic. But, is this *mere* awareness of one's finitude what characterizes Dasein's authenticity? No, authenticity consists in *allowing* one's awareness of finitude to delineate the multiplicity of one's possibilities and as such become existentially self-possessed. It is a bursting forth of possibility, and a further answer to the call toward existential self-possession, not a *mere* awareness of finitude. This, however, is not the unfolding series of events for suicidal-Dasein. For suicidal-Dasein, its awareness of finitude does *not* open it up to the multiplicity of its possibilities, rather, suicidal-Dasein remains fixated on the one possibility of its own self-inflicted impossibility—namely, suicidal-Dasein's desire to end its own life, to pull itself into oblivion.

For this reason, the *choice* to commit suicide and the *act* of suicide itself must be inauthentic. It fails to achieve existential self-possession as a result of a narrowing of Dasein's awareness of its possibilities to the one *self-annihilating possibility*—the complete and final self-inflicted annihilation of Dasein's possibilities itself. This is evidently an avoidance of the call to one's existential freedom and responsibility. But, it is also inauthentic because the narrowing of Dasein's awareness of its possibilities to the singular possibility also dissolves the *belief* in the very concept of *choice*—for in choice, Dasein must be aware of at least two possibilities. If you are aware of Pepsi as being the only beverage available, do you believe you have a choice of what you are going to drink? You might say, "I can choose not to drink," and that *that* is two possibilities. But, as we will see, even Dasein's awareness of the possibility of *refraining* from the definitive suicidal action is closed in some cases—this occurs when Dasein has become completely deceived into believing that suicide is the *only* option and is in the very process of carrying out the act, due to a false belief in the *necessity* of the act. Similarly, your unbearable pangs of thirst might deceive you into believing that you *have* to drink the Pepsi in order to alleviate the pangs of thirst you feel. It is the result of a psychological process that transforms one's belief of possibility into illusory necessity. Thus, in avoiding the call to existential self-possession, in the further alteration in the *awareness* that Dasein has about its possibilities, and in the dissolve of Dasein's *belief* in choice itself, suicide is revealed as an inauthentic mode of being.

-----------∽∞∾-----------

SUFFERING

What leads to Dasein's suicidal ideation and eventual suicide? Before we attempt an answer to this question, it will be necessary to outline what is meant by *inextricable contingency*. There are parts of the world that Dasein is thrown into that are contingent—namely, that the president of the United States is different for Dasein today than it was for Dasein fifty years ago, that the rules and laws Dasein is held accountable for are different now than they were two hundred years ago, and so on. These contingencies are subject to change. What I call an *inextricable contingency* is something that transcends the context, history, and time of the world, and thus it is a phenomenon that is experienced by all Dasein at some point. However, it remains a contingency because of *how* the phenomenon manifests—namely, it is subject to change from culture to culture, context to context, history to history, and so on.

An example of an inextricable contingency would be morality—the project of defining *what actions are good and what actions are bad*, or, similarly, the project of defining *what has value and what does not*. The whole of human history has been tied up with these moral questions, and Dasein cannot escape this project—*all* Dasein at *all* times have valued some things, while not valuing others and have also defined various actions, thoughts, words, practices, and objects as either good or bad. However, *what* is considered good or bad and *what* is valued or not valued is contingent—namely, subject to change from culture to culture, history to history, and context to context. This of course is not to make a claim about cultural relativism—it is simply to say that what humans value or do not value and what humans *believe* is good or bad change, but the project of morality is perpetual, and thus *inextricable*.

Suffering as an Inextricable Contingency

Now we can answer the question: *What leads to Dasein's suicidal ideation and eventual suicide?* People take their own lives because they believe that *Nothing is better than Being*, that self-annihilation is the only possibility in the face of an unbearable and unrelenting suffering that cannot be justified. In some way, then, *suffering* must be the phenomenon that closes Dasein's awareness of their possibilities within the multiplicity to one. More precisely, suffering must *alter* Dasein's relation to its multiplicity. The way that suffering does this is by injecting three *illusions*[2] into

---

[2] Making the claim that people who are suicidal are also people that are conditioned by certain illusions or irrationalities regarding the nature of suffering should not be of a contentious or controversial point of view. Usually, our initial reaction to people who are suicidal is to attempt to bring them to a hospital whereby they can talk to a psychiatrist or psychologist who specializes [continued on next page]

Dasein—which can be defined as a false belief. An attempt will thus be made to elucidate 1) how these three illusions emerge from out of the phenomenon of suffering and 2) how these illusions, alongside suffering, ultimately facilitate this psychological *narrowing process.*

Suffering is an inextricable contingency of the world that Dasein has been thrown into, which serves to turn Dasein away from its multiplicity of possibilities, and thus also away from its authenticity. *All* Dasein have and will suffer—*how* and *how much* they will suffer is subject to contingency. And yet, to overwhelmingly suffer is to both stray away from the choice to continue the project of essence defining and turn toward finitude (our ownmost death), but in this case, as a *potential escape.* This turn toward finitude as a potential escape from Dasein's own unfolding trajectory through the multiplicity of possibilities is in conflict with Heidegger's view that a turning toward finitude is the source of existential self-possession. The former is a closing of Dasein's awareness of its possibilities, while the latter is an opening of Dasein's awareness of its possibilities.

However, these two ways that Dasein can turn toward its finitude are not incompatible, and thus pose no serious threat to Heidegger's analysis. Rather, what is called for is a broadening of the possible ways that Dasein can look toward finitude. This is intuitive once laid out in simpler terms. Thinking about our approaching death and thus the fact that we are fleeting beings can do one of two things. It can either motivate our existential journey in relentlessly carving out what we want to become, or it can make

---

[from previous page] in dismantling various illusions occupying people who suffer from mental illnesses or who have developed an unhealthy relationship with the nature of suffering. This initial response should reveal our intuitive belief that suicidal ideation is usually a derivative of states of mind that are unhealthy and irrational (namely, false beliefs about the nature of suffering). This is not to say that all people who are suicidal suffer from mental illness—quite the contrary. However, people *can* be conditioned by various false beliefs without fitting the diagnostic criteria for a mental illness.

us long for the *quiet goodnight*—death, annihilation, and the impossibility of Dasein. In longing for the quiet goodnight, suicidal ideation begins. This longing is Dasein *pulling-towards-itself* its own inevitable impossibility. Perhaps Heidegger purposely omitted the fact that Dasein can long for the relief it believes will come with self-annihilation because in addition to anxiety, Dasein can also *cherish* the facticity of its own finitude insofar as Dasein can become *grateful* of its own condition as a *finite* being. This makes *longing* and *cherishing* both another *mood* [*Stimmung*] toward death, moods that both contrast with anxiety.

Degree and Psychological Interpretation

But, still, this analysis of suffering is not deep enough. It has yet to be outlined *how* suffering deceives Dasein into believing that the multiplicity must be reduced to one possibility. Here is precisely how the phenomena unfold. At first, Dasein is aware of the multiplicity of possibilities that are presented with every dawning moment, in which Dasein must choose and ultimately become. Because suffering is an inextricable contingency of Dasein, some of these possibilities, in their manifestation, will accompany some degree of suffering—if I choose to play football, I could break my leg, if I choose to have a girlfriend, I could end up heartbroken, and so on. Now, the manifestation of suffering is an inevitability for Dasein at some point along its trajectory through the multiplicity—but, both the *degree* of suffering that manifests for each Dasein and the *psychological interpretation* that Dasein has toward the inevitability of suffering differs in important ways from one Dasein to the next. These differences condition Dasein's degree of susceptibility to each of the three illusions. Thus, these differences must be elucidated, for in this elucidation the illusions that condition suicidal-Dasein will become revealed.

First, each Dasein differs in the degree of suffering that manifests in the course of their life. Most Dasein experience normal and expected degrees of suffering in the trajectory of their life (eventual passing of loved ones, some financial hardships, heartbreak, ultimate physical illness, death at an old age, and so on). Much fewer Dasein, however, suffer from unluckier fates and experience *more* than expected degrees of suffering. Let us call these individuals *unlucky-Dasein.*

Second, each Dasein psychologically interprets the inevitability of suffering in different ways. Most Dasein do so in a *healthy manner*—recognizing that some future possibilities within the multiplicity will contain suffering while a greater number of possibilities *will not* contain any suffering at all. In stark contrast, a high proportion of unlucky-Dasein develop an *unhealthy* psychological interpretation toward their possibilities. Namely, unlucky-Dasein interprets the *majority* of its possibilities as containing suffering. This is similarly the case for *depressed-Dasein,* who does not necessarily have to have experienced the same heightened degree of suffering as unlucky-Dasein (though they certainly may have and perhaps even more so), but rather is conditioned by psychologically irrational interpretive structures regarding the nature of the relationship between suffering and the possibilities within its multiplicity (they *overestimate* the degree of suffering within the world, they are hyper-sensitive to their suffering insofar as they magnify it, and so on). This is aligned with Aaron Beck's theory of depression and his cognitive triad model.[3]

[1]   The First Illusion

It is in Dasein's psychological interpretation of this relationship

---

[3] This is certainly not a comprehensive encapsulation of the psychological phenomenon of depression, or even of Aaron Beck's cognitive theory of depression. Rather, it is just to demonstrate that people who are depressed can and do develop and become conditioned by irrational schemas about the world, the self, and the future. In this specific case, we are talking about the irrational schemas regarding the nature of suffering that can develop and ultimately condition people who are depressed.

that the first illusion can take hold of unlucky-Dasein and depressed-Dasein, pushing them closer to suicidal-Dasein. Namely, over time both unlucky-Dasein and depressed-Dasein begin to believe that suffering is an *essential property* of each and every possibility within the multiplicity that is presented with every moment—that *every single possibility* must necessarily consist of some degree of suffering. They begin to see suffering in the same way that death is seen by authentic Dasein—*as an essential property of Dasein itself* (I may become a doctor or a lawyer, but no matter what I choose to become, I will indefinitely and perpetually suffer). But, this is the illusion—the belief that there cannot exist a possibility devoid of suffering.

Here it is important to clarify again the concept of *multiplicity of possibilities*. Every single moment presents a multiplicity for Dasein. This multiplicity consists of innumerable possibilities (ways of being) from which Dasein chooses *one* to actualize. In any given moment, I have a *range* of possible actions I can take, thoughts I can have, words I can say, and so on (I can say this or that, I can do this or that, or I can think this or that). These are my *possibilities*. Out of which I choose *one*, and thus it *becomes* part of my essence.

Suicidal-Dasein's belief that *each and every possibility within each presented multiplicity is conditioned by the property of essential suffering* is an illusion. This is a false belief as it derives from a misinterpretation of the relationship between suffering and the innumerable possibilities within the multiplicity insofar as there *always do exist* possibilities without suffering in the trajectory of Dasein's life.[4] This is not contentious unless one believes

---

4 There is, however, a rare exception to this. For a select few *very* unlucky-Dasein suffering *does* become an *essential property of each and every possibility*. We can readily think of those among us diagnosed with terrible, incurable, and terminal illnesses that produce perpetual suffering (i.e., diseases like ALS—think Stephen Hawking, or certain cancers requiring heavy doses of chemo and radiation therapy, and so on). Let us call these cases *incurable-Dasein*. In such cases, it would be far more difficult to claim that incurable-Dasein, who then becomes suicidal-Dasein, is one conditioned by the illusion stated above. For, in the case of incurable-Dasein they *actually are* conditioned by essential suffering! Most of us might even be sympathetic to their physician-assisted suicide—and see incurable-Dasein's decision to pull-towards-itself its [continued on next page]

that depression and other forms of mental suffering cannot be reasonably managed, or that physical suffering does not at points subside, or that at any given moment a person cannot experience laughter, love, and the warmth and care of family, friends and loved ones (not to mention a multitude of other possibilities that carry no degree of suffering). Keep in mind that the illusion consists of unlucky-Dasein's and depressed-Dasein's belief that the possibilities stated above are *impossibilities*. It is certainly possible that unlucky-Dasein's and depressed-Dasein's *actual* trajectory through the multiplicity continues to be perpetually suffering *because* they can no longer see possibilities without suffering and thus cannot think to bring them into Being. This does not detract from the fact that those possibilities *are there,* that unlucky-Dasein and depressed-Dasein *could* possibly see a psychiatrist, or *could* possibly take medication, or *could* possibly talk to their family, friends, and loved ones, and so on. But these possibilities remain veiled in the first illusion conditioning unlucky-Dasein and depressed-Dasein, causing them to believe that suffering is ceaseless—that suffering is *perpetual.*

[2]   The Second Illusion

Next, unlucky-Dasein and depressed-Dasein must make a choice. They can learn to *justify* their condition as suffering beings, or alternatively, they can decide to reject the project of justification. This rejection is a *rebellion* against the phenomenon of suffering and against Dasein's condition as the very conduit for the phenomenon of suffering. The former choice (learning to justify) can pull unlucky-Dasein and depressed-Dasein from out of the initial illusion that suffering is an essential property of each and every

---

[from previous page] own inevitable impossibility as one that is justified. However, for the purposes of this essay, my focus here will remain on suicidal-Dasein conditioned by the *illusion* of essential suffering—insofar as cases of incurable-Dasein are far rarer and represent a smaller proportion of people who take their own lives.

possibility within the multiplicity. The latter choice (rejection of the project of justification) pushes unlucky-Dasein and depressed-Dasein closer toward a complete psychological transformation into suicidal-Dasein, for in the latter choice, the second illusion develops. This occurs when unlucky-Dasein's and depressed-Dasein's rebellion against a multiplicity of possibilities that is believed to be conditioned by an essential property of suffering takes on the form of a false rationalization that their own suffering *cannot be justified.* This illusion can be easily understood from a psychological perspective, given that they feel a strong urge to avoid justifying the thing they want *least* justified—*their suffering.* It is the product of extreme cognitive dissonance. Under this lens, it can make psychological sense why unlucky-Dasein and depressed-Dasein inevitably rationalize themselves into the illusion that their suffering *cannot be justified,* for in choosing to justify their suffering they first have to admit that their suffering *ought to be justified.* For many, this is simply too difficult a feat.

[3]   The Third Illusion

It is at this point that the narrowing process within Dasein unfolds as unlucky-Dasein and depressed-Dasein begin their search for any possibility that *is* devoid of suffering. They then happen upon the one and only possibility that promises to dissolve suffering altogether—*Dasein's ownmost death.* Death becomes, what they believe, is their only potential escape from a multiplicity of possibilities conditioned by the illusion of essential and unjustified suffering. Insofar as this process unfolds, unlucky-Dasein and depressed-Dasein transform into suicidal-Dasein. At this moment, the moods of *longing* and *cherishing* toward finitude manifest, and suicidal-Dasein closes up to all other possibilities in a profound defiance of the multiplicity. Suicidal-Dasein then obsessively ruminates, thinking itself into the third and final illusion that self-annihilation *is its only possibility.* In doing so, suicidal-Dasein develops the misguided belief that this possibility is *necessity*. Consequently, Dasein turns away from the multiplicity becoming truly inauthentic. This is when choice *appears* to dissolve, when possibilities narrow to a *seemingly* hopeless one, and when suicidal-Dasein believes it *must* follow through and commit itself to the act of suicide.

A Summary of Suffering

This is the delineation of how suffering closes Dasein's awareness of its possibilities to one. When suffering becomes too great to bear, Dasein loses the capacity to be anxious in the face of finitude, substituting anxiety with the moods of *cherishing* and *longing.* In the moment when the pain of choosing becomes more dreadful than the anxiety of finitude, annihilation, and impossibility, suffering alters Dasein's belief about the magnitude of its multiplicity of possibilities. Dasein's multiplicity then *appears* to dwindle to the singular self-annihilating possibility. This is the consequence of being conditioned by these three false beliefs. Namely, that suffering is an essential property of each and every possibility within one's multiplicity, that one's suffering cannot be justified, and that ultimately self-annihilation is one's only possibility.

Suicidal-Dasein is acutely aware of the eternal relief accompanying the complete and final dissolution of its Being from the world, that to dissolve into impossibility is to escape suffering. Unfortunately, suicidal-Dasein is also conditioned by the various illusions previously stated. Of course, it *is* true that suffering is an inextricable contingency of human existence, but this is not to say that *every* possible way of being for Dasein consists of a suffering, that suffering *cannot at all* be justified, and that self-annihilation is the *only* possibility—clearly this is not the case. Yet, suicidal-Dasein remains mistaken about the features of the phenomenon of human suffering, considering it to be a *perpetual and unjustified condition* of human existence, instead of as an inextricable contingency with the potential for justification and avoidance. The fact remains that there are many moments in Dasein's temporal trajectory that are devoid of suffering, there are many facets of existence that provide justification for our lives as suffering beings, and there are many choices to make other than suicide. This raises the question: *Is there an inextricable contingency of the world into which Dasein has been thrown that opens Dasein's belief in the number of possibilities it has, even when finitude no longer will?*

BEAUTY

Suicidal-Dasein can no longer look toward death and finitude for an opening up of its possibilities. This is because, in the eyes of suicidal-Dasein, death is seen as a relieving escape rather than a looming Sword of Damocles. As a result, it appears as though suicidal-Dasein is blinded from the call toward existential self-possession. But, this is incompatible with the fact that sometimes suicidal-Dasein chooses *against* suicide, opting for life instead. For these reasons, there must exist something other than its own finitude that opens up, before the eyes of suicidal-Dasein, its multiplicity of possibilities, and also presents the call toward authenticity.

The most readily available phenomenon that comes to mind is beauty. For one, it also transcends context, history, and time—insofar as *all* Dasein at *all* times have perceived and made judgments of beauty. This makes it an *inextricable contingency*, similar to the phenomenon of suffering. Intuitively, beauty seems to be the perfect candidate. But, it must be determined if beauty is *that* inextricable contingency that can open up suicidal-Dasein's awareness toward its multiplicity of possibilities, away from the one annihilating possibility that suicidal-Dasein fixates on.

From experience, we know how powerful it can be to behold something beautiful. People the world over talk of the power of beauty to transform and bring people back from bouts of depression, sadness, and nihilism. This gives us an intuitive sense of the power of beauty in helping us transcend suffering. But, how does beauty open up Dasein's awareness?

A Deeper Analysis: Being Beholden

The beautiful *grips* us, meaning that we do not experience an aesthetic judgment of beauty through our own volition—I cannot simply decide of my own free will to experience beauty while looking at my plain, wooden desk or my carpeted, beige floor. Rather, beautiful scenes and objects in the external world take hold of our cognitive faculties without consent.

It is in this peculiar quality of being beholden to beauty that we are to find how beauty opens up suicidal-Dasein's awareness of its possibilities, and furthermore, how beauty calls upon suicidal-Dasein to authentically take up the project of existential self-possession.

Suicidal-Dasein is non-consensually gripped by the beautiful—by some magnificent sublimity of the world into which Dasein has been thrown (a serene landscape, a colourful sunset, an emotionally salient song, and so on). In this moment, suicidal-Dasein's awareness opens up. The peculiar feature of this moment is that this aesthetic gripping of the beautiful tilts the probability of Dasein's unfolding choice toward an affirmation of life—namely, by both luring Dasein to unwittingly revel instead of self-annihilate, and by disclosing the illusions as illusions. In reveling, Dasein's entire multiplicity of possibilities flashes before Dasein in a profound delineation—bringing forth again the option to answer the call of existential self-possession and authenticity. The question becomes, *how?*

Outlining the Taxonomy of Suffering

Before this question can be answered, it will be important to sketch an outline of the division of suffering for Dasein. The first half of the division of suffering for Dasein is *physical suffering*. Physical suffering can take on many forms (i.e., burns, broken bones, pinches, dull-aches, cuts, bruises, swelling, hunger pangs, suffocation, and so on). However, these can all be classified under the rubric of physical suffering insofar as they are all *physical sensations*. The second half of the division of suffering for Dasein is *mental suffering*. Similarly, mental suffering can take on many forms (i.e., grief, sorrow, heartache, despair, sadness, melancholy, feelings of worthlessness, betrayal, unhappiness, depression, spiritual and existential crises, and so on). However, these can all be classified under the rubric of *mental suffering* insofar as they are all manifestations of the mind (mental products). The point made here is that the totality of human suffering can be catalogued into the two halves of this division. This division is important to keep in mind given that the way each half of the division interacts with beauty is slightly different. Nonetheless, regardless of *how* suicidal-Dasein suffers (whether physically or mentally), beauty always carries the capacity to present the call of existential self-possession and authenticity, such that *every* form of suffering (both physical and mental) is brought to its knees in Dasein's confrontations with beauty. Now we are able to answer the previously posed question: *How does being beholden to beauty bring forth the option to answer the call of existential self-possession and authenticity in suicidal-Dasein?*

[1]   The First Power of Being Beholden to Beauty

The first revelation that suicidal-Dasein is immediately struck by in its aesthetic judgment of beauty is *the possibility of having*

more than one possibility—more than the possibility of self-anni-
hilation. More specifically, in this moment, suicidal-Dasein is
forcefully confronted with *two possibilities*. The first is to con-
tinue along the path toward self-annihilation, while the second is
to halt the path of self-annihilation in exchange for *reveling* in the
phenomenon of beauty (a previously ignored possibility). This
first power of being beholden to beauty is a major blow to the
third illusion conditioning suicidal-Dasein that *self-annihilation
is the only possibility* because it is a visceral demonstration that
suicide is not a necessity. This particular power of being beholden
to beauty is inclusive of both halves of the division of suffering.
Meaning that both physically suffering suicidal-Dasein *and* men-
tally suffering suicidal-Dasein will have this revelation in being
beholden to beauty.

[2]   The Second Power of Being Beholden to Beauty

Secondly, in suicidal-Dasein's simultaneous experience of beauty
and suffering, suicidal-Dasein is forcefully made aware of the
possibility of being justified in its existence as a *suffering being*.
In suicidal-Dasein's aesthetic judgment of beauty, an instinctual,
immediate, and pre-rational justification for Dasein's existence as
a suffering being is internally felt in the form of an affirmation of
Being over Nothingness, an affirmation of life over death. This
second power of being beholden to beauty exerts yet another ma-
jor blow to an illusion conditioning suicidal-Dasein. Namely, a
blow to the illusion that *Dasein's condition as a suffering being
cannot be justified.*

Another characteristic of this particular power of being be-
holden to beauty is that it serves to *existentially alleviate* the
suffering of suicidal-Dasein, insofar as justified suffering is more
bearable than unjustified suffering. This alleviation is existential
and psychological, rather than physical (though, its capacity to re-
duce physiological measures of suffering is not entirely out of the

question). Similarly, this particular power of being beholden to beauty is *also* inclusive of both halves of the division of suffering. Both physically and mentally suffering suicidal-Dasein will have this revelation in being beholden to beauty.

[3] The Third Power of Being Beholden to Beauty

The third power of being beholden to beauty depends on the nature of suicidal-Dasein's suffering. Namely, in these involuntary confrontations with the beautiful, *mentally* suffering suicidal-Dasein is made aware of a possibility within the multiplicity that is *without* suffering. In Dasein's continued reveling in beauty, certain forms of *mental* suffering are dissolved (even if only for a brief moment). As a result, this experience forcefully demonstrates within Dasein the existence of a possibility that is without suffering. This is the consequence of our aesthetic judgments of beauty being a contemplative and mental enterprise, serving to take up *mental real-estate* within suicidal-Dasein. Insofar as mental real-estate is filled, suicidal-Dasein's mental suffering is quieted for a brief moment, so long as suicidal-Dasein continues to be beholden to beauty. This goes directly against the first illusion that *suffering is an essential property of each and every possibility within the multiplicity*. As a result of the third power, suffering is reverted back to an inextricable contingency—though still inevitable, mentally suffering suicidal-Dasein realizes that suffering is not *perpetual,* that it is not an *essential property of each and every possibility.*

Once again, this particular feature of Dasein's experience of beauty is contingent upon the *type* of suffering experienced—and is specifically reserved for forms of mental suffering, not physical suffering. For suicidal-Dasein that physically suffers, beauty cannot simply *dissolve* their felt suffering; rather it can only justify it, serving to existentially alleviate it. If I break your arm while you are beholden to beauty, being beholden to beauty will not *dissolve* the pain in your arm, thus for suicidal-Dasein that physically suffers, a blow to the illusion of suffering as an essential property will arise much later in their recovery.[5]

The caveat made for the third power of being beholden to beauty (as being reserved for mental suffering) should not detract from the magnitude of this power, considering the astonishingly high rate of people that suffer *solely* from mental illnesses (300 million people globally suffer from major depressive disorder alone [*World Health Organization*, 2018], not to mention the number of people who have or will suffer from *any* mental illness or mental problem at some point in their lifetime, which skyrockets into the *billions* [*World Health Organization*, 2018]).

Beauty's Call Toward Authenticity

As previously alluded to, it only takes *one* of these illusions to be revealed as an illusion for suicidal-Dasein to become aware that *it was mistaken* about the features characterizing the multiplicity of possibilities.[6] The peculiar nature of being beholden to beauty is that its first and second power will *always* reveal their respective illusions as illusions for suicidal-Dasein as a result of each power being inclusive of all forms of suffering. Nevertheless, as a result of being struck by these revelations, a *reanalysis* of the

---

[5] This is obviously not the case for Dasein diagnosed with incurable illnesses that produce *perpetual* suffering (such as ALS). They can never reveal this illusion as illusion because for incurable-Dasein it is *not* an illusion. Nonetheless, the first and second power of being beholden to beauty are still at play for incurable-Dasein, and thus, still presents the call to existential self-possession and authenticity. This is not to make any claim for or against the moral status of physician-assisted suicide.

[6] It seems entirely possible that there exist other phenomena within the world that would also reveal these three illusions as illusions—laughter, meaning, purpose, family, God, and so on. But, in my analysis, I have focused on being beholden to beauty because of its peculiar ability to reveal *all* illusions that condition suicidal-Dasein as illusions, insofar as the caveat for the third power is met.

multiplicity of possibilities transpires in Dasein. In this reanalysis, suicidal-Dasein is struck by the possibility of reinterpreting the world into which it was thrown as not being *all suffering, all the time,* as being a place that can reasonably justify any suffering that may inevitably appear, and as being a place where suicidal-Dasein does not *have* to commit suicide.

In Dasein's reanalysis of the multiplicity—due to a realization of its being mistaken about the multiplicity on three levels—its possibilities are necessarily brought before its eyes, thus revealing the type of being that Dasein is—*a free, finite who.* For suicidal-Dasein, this can be a breakthrough moment moving it toward authenticity—*'I could live for one more day, just to experience the beauty of the world,' 'I could call my parents and tell them I love them,' 'I could see a psychiatrist,'* and *'In these choices, I may not suffer, and yet, even if I do continue to suffer, I now have the justificatory means to live with my condition as a suffering being.'* For these reasons, a *reveling* in beauty is a *fundamental mood* [*Grundstimmung*], insofar as it calls upon Dasein to become existentially self-possessed and authentic. In Dasein's recovery, it may even begin to look back upon death again with the anxiety that Heidegger spoke of because it is now aware of possibilities to *live for.*

This of course is not *always* what happens. It is also possible for suicidal-Dasein to self-annihilate regardless of its involuntary confrontation with beauty and the subsequent dissolve of its illusions. For we must never forget the ferocity of our merciless opponent: *human suffering.* The point here is that in being beholden to beauty two possibilities *do* arise, the illusions *are* revealed,[7] and then, as a result, the very delineation of the multiplicity of suicidal-Dasein's possibilities is laid out. Dasein is then confronted with a *choice: either inauthentically commit suicide or authentically revel in beauty.*

---

[7] Two illusions for *physical* suffering and all three illusions for *mental* suffering.

⌐∽⌐

CONCLUSION

In my reading of Martin Heidegger's *Being and Time*, I was surprised by the omission of suffering and suicide in his hyperrigorous account of Dasein, of Dasein's relationship to the world, and of Dasein's relationship to the question of Being. Heidegger asks the question—*'Why are there beings at all instead of nothing?'*—and gives this question ontological significance, insofar as it is a question that is only a concern for Dasein. Another question of ontological significance—*'Is Being better than Nothing?'*—was one that was not discussed in Heidegger's seminal *Being and Time*. This moral question of ontology—moral insofar as it is a question that is a value judgment—ought to be considered in any delineation of Dasein, for Dasein, gripped by this question, with the presence of overwhelming and inextricably contingent suffering, moves itself toward self-annihilation—with self-annihilation being an inauthentic mode of being toward finitude. With this in mind, it is unclear why Heidegger spoke not of suffering and suicide.

—JEREMY FORSYTHE

If you are having thoughts of suicide, please call the suicide prevention lifeline. There is more to life than suffering.

National Lifeline for the US: 1-800-273-8255
National Lifeline for Canada: 1-833-456-4566
For International Lifelines, visit www.suicide.org

REFERENCE LIST

[1] Heidegger, M., Fried, G., & Polt, R. (2014). *Introduction to metaphysics*. New Haven: Yale University Press.

[2] Camus, A. (2000). *The myth of Sisyphus*. London: Penguin.

[3] (n.d.). Retrieved from http://www.who.int/en

[4] (n.d.). Retrieved from http://nws.merriam-webster.com/open-dictionary/

[5] (n.d.). Retrieved from https://plato.stanford.edu/

[6] (n.d.). Retrieved from https://www.britannica.com/

[7] Critchley, S. (2009). *Being and time, part 1: Why Heidegger matters*. The Guardian. Retrieved from https://www.theguardian.com

[8] Critchley, S. (2009). *Being and time, part 2: On 'mineness.'* The Guardian. Retrieved from https://www.theguardian.com

[9] Critchley, S. (2009). *Being and time, part 3: On 'being-in-the-world.'* The Guardian. Retrieved from https://www.theguardian.com

[10] Critchley, S. (2009). *Being and time, part 4: On 'thrown into this world.'* The Guardian. Retrieved from https://www.theguardian.com

[11] Critchley, S. (2009). *Being and time, part 5: On 'anxiety.'* The Guardian. Retrieved from https://www.theguardian.com

[12] Critchley, S. (2009). *Being and time, part 6: On 'death.'* The Guardian. Retrieved from https://www.theguardian.com

[13] Mulhall, S. (1996). *Routledge philosophy guidebook to Heidegger and being and time*. London: Routledge.

[14] Dreyfus, H. L. (2009). *Being-in-the-world: A commentary on Heidegger's being and time, division I*. Cambridge. Mass. u.a.: MIT Press.

[15] Heidegger, M. (2013). *Being and time*. United States: Stellar Books.

[16] Kaufmann, W. A. (1960). *Existentialism from Dostoevsky to Sartre*. New York: Meridian Books.

[17] Thoreau, H. D. (2003). *A week on the concord and merrimack rivers*. The Penn State University Electronic Classics Series.

ACKNOWLEDGMENTS

To my mom, for all of the impromptu psychology and philosophy lectures you've had to endure. Thank you for your continued support. You are my rock.

To my beautiful girlfriend, Melika, for being so accepting of my moments of creative mania. I love you.

To my brilliant best friends. Oh, the ups and downs we've had. But, how worth it, if only for all of the satiating conversations.

To my future children, my father taught me to cast a line into still waters, and I will teach you the same.

To my favourite professors, and to those of antiquity, how you've stirred my eyes and heart, how you've believed in my potential.

And finally, a special thank you to my readers.

INDEX

ABOUT THE AUTHOR

Jeremy Forsythe is an aspiring writer, philosopher, and future clinical psychologist.

He graduated with an Honours Bachelor of science degree at the University of Toronto, specializing in psychology and philosophy. He is currently in the process of pursuing an MA, and then PhD, in clinical psychology.

His research interests focus on the logical structures of nihilism (feelings of purposelessness, meaninglessness, and aimlessness), and their potential for alleviation using bibliotherapies, and a further focus on the potential for judgments of beauty to alleviate mental, physical, and psychological distress.

Jeremy's poetry explores themes of suicide, philosophy, beauty, art, creativity, nihilism, existentialism, human psychology, and one's choice of life over death, of Being over Nothing.

His first book, *Doves and Dasein,* is an anthology of aphorisms that attempts to elucidate his experience living as a human, utterly aware of the peculiarity of the human condition.

Currently, he has finished two novels that explore the same themes. One that explores the psychology of a man completely ailed by the presence of an indifferent universe. While the other is about a man stranded in the middle of a barren desert with no hope of escape. These novels are still in the process of publication.

Connect with Jeremy Forsythe on Instagram, where he posts exclusive aphorisms.

@jeremy.forsythe
#jforsythe #dovesanddasein

Made in the USA
Lexington, KY
26 September 2018